KT-433-723

One of the Family

One of the Family

*Why a Dog Called Maxwell
Changed My Life*

NICKY CAMPBELL

HODDER &
STOUGHTON

First published in Great Britain in 2021 by Hodder & Stoughton
An Hachette UK company

2

Family photo, p. 110 © Nick Harvey Photography Ltd;
Into the night, p. 94 © Sarah Louise Ramsay Photography.
All other pictures © Author's collection.

A CIP catalogue record for this title is available from the British Library

Hardback ISBN 978 1 529 30425 1
eBook ISBN 978 1 529 30426 8

Typeset in Celeste by Palimpsest Book Production Ltd, Falkirk, Stirlingshire

Printed and bound in Great Britain by Clays Ltd, Elcograf S.p.A.

Hodder & Stoughton policy is to use papers that are natural, renewable
and recyclable products and made from wood grown in sustainable forests.
The logging and manufacturing processes are expected to conform to
the environmental regulations of the country of origin.

Hodder & Stoughton Ltd
Carmelite House
50 Victoria Embankment
London EC4Y ODZ

www.hodder.co.uk

To my mum, Sheila Campbell

My Boy

Thirty-Five Wasted Years

WE'D RUN UP a mountain track above the sea loch and down to its shore and now, on our way back, the sun glinting on the water, I felt this overwhelming urge to cool down. Leaping into the river, I hit the water with a glorious ice-cold explosion. My mind was clearing.

As I floated up for air, I felt something yanking on my soaking-wet T-shirt, dragging me sideways. Frantic with panic, Maxwell had jumped in after me and was now pulling me to safety. I swam to the edge and climbed out, Maxwell following. Collapsing onto the bank, I lay back on the grass and he licked my face, welcoming me back to the land of the living. And as I looked into the loving innocence of his brown eyes, I felt so fortunate that he was mine. His instinct was, with every last drop of strength, to save me. And he did. Not then, from the river – although he was convinced of it – but later from the torrent that was to overwhelm me.

I love it when people ask what we did to deserve dogs. I love it because there is no answer – only awe, wonder and a shrugging acceptance of our inadequacies.

For thirty-five wasted years I didn't have a dog. Only the

dogs of others; of friends, acquaintances and strangers. I didn't truly realise how much I yearned for one – until Maxwell, my molten-golden Labrador, arrived, and then it all came flooding back. I remembered the comfort and security that had come from my childhood dog, Candy, and I remembered the precious privilege of loving an animal and being loved in return.

Candy was gone but always somewhere. Long after he was put to 'sleep' he dwelt in mine; in my dreams. And then twelve years ago Maxwell arrived, not a moment too soon. We've been inseparable since then, our bond visceral and strong. But it's not just the bond between me and Maxwell that's been of such comfort. He has helped me focus on the other bonds that really matter to me and over the last few years, I've found myself surprised at what I've discovered. You can so easily see the world in a certain way and claim the truth as your own but then, with the remarkable, unspoken bond, the love and tenderness of a dog and the love and tenderness of loving a dog, everything can just change.

In 2004, I wrote about my adoption search in *Blue-Eyed Son*, as I traced my birth mother and birth father, and I thought I was closer to self-revelation. But in reality, I wasn't an inch nearer to understanding anything. That account was essentially a detective story. I was solving a mystery and, like a journalist reporting on someone else's story, I was intoxicated by the *process* but essentially detached from the consequences. Questions were answered – who, what, where and when – but that was all. Nothing about finding out who they were touched the core of me, the lifelong trauma of being an imposter in my own life; the true me, unknown and unreachable.

Nor did knowing who my birth mother was do anything to quell my unresolved issues with the woman or 'mother' who gave me away. For here's the nonsense that makes perfect sense: in giving me up for adoption, she ensured I went on to a better life than she could ever have given me. For this I'm grateful and would never have wanted it any other way. My parents are my parents. I don't have enough words to say how special they were and how happy my childhood was. Or how lucky I am to be their child. And yet, I could still hear the incessant undercurrent rumbling beneath me. That lifelong whisper coming from inside me: she didn't want you, she didn't want you, she gave you away, you were no good.

It's taken a long long time to stop listening to that tune in my head and it's still not entirely quietened. But since I began presenting *Long Lost Family* in 2009, I've found myself in extraordinary places, meeting and talking intimately with dozens of adopted sons and daughters with the same feelings and similar stories, and the soundtrack has shifted. The adopted children I've met have, without exception, been possessed of an emotional eloquence that I've never had. It's as though I'm looking in the mirror, hearing variations on a theme that unites us, and after so many years now of listening carefully, I have come to learn what I didn't think I even needed to understand, and I now realise was too afraid to try: the true perspective of the birth mother. The hurt, the grief and the fight to just live again.

Something switched on in my heart when Maxwell

arrived. He came along at exactly the right time in my life. My mum – my adoptive mum – always used to say it was clear, once she and my dad adopted me, that it was meant to be. Our family was, for her, perfect in its completeness – Mum, Dad, my sister Fiona and me. We'd all found each other in this universe. For me, it was the same – my wife Tina, my four glorious children and then, twelve years ago, like a meteor, Maxwell. He landed and has never left my side. When things were going off the rails and unresolved issues needed resolving, he helped me – he was by my side in wild, weird and wonderful places.

My relationship with Maxwell liberates and renews me, because in that space we share, he lets me off the lead and I can break free, escape from the deafening cacophony all around. He clears my mind and frees my spirit. He knows only truth; he inhabits only the present. When I was a little boy and when unhappy feelings sometimes took over, Candy was always there for me. Knowing exactly who I was. And so does this boy Maxwell. He knows *exactly* who I am – so he's got one over on me there. And, he licks my face.

As I was writing this book, Mum died at the age of ninety-six. During the course of the year we'd had several conversations about my early life and in particular my most faithful childhood friend, Candy. She also helped me see the long view and overcome the enormous feelings of guilt I'd internalised when I'd traced my birth mother, despite her supportive acceptance that I needed to know who she was. This, in turn, along with *Long Lost Family*, my family and Maxwell helped me redefine my thinking about Stella,

4

my birth mother, and – thirty years later – to do something I never thought I'd be able to do.

Mum is the person I wanted to see this book most of all, and I only wish she was here to read what my stuttering, spluttering self has, until now, been unable to adequately express.

This book is for you, Mum.

*Mum, Candy and me at the window of our house
in Mayfield Road, 1965*

CHAPTER ONE

Mowgli of Midlothian

I'VE ALWAYS KNOWN I was adopted. Mum – my adopted mother – gave my birth mother rave reviews and I was alert to the story of my creation. It went something like this: my birth mother was a nurse and very good at her job; in fact, she was so good at her job that she was put in charge of all the other nurses at the hospital and everybody liked working with her. When she discovered she was pregnant she realised that she wouldn't be able to look after her baby when he was born because she had a very busy job, caring for sick people until they were better. So she came all the way over by boat from Ireland to Edinburgh, where she knew some people who would help her find the best family to take care of her baby and give him the most loving home.

At the same time my mum and dad were looking for a baby. They'd already had one, who was now five years old, but after she was born they hadn't been able to have another child. When my mum had talked to her doctor, he'd told her about a mother who wanted another mother to have her baby, so he put two and one together and made four.

When I was born my birth mother chose the name Nicholas for me and she looked after me for nine days in

Edinburgh in the house of the people she knew. Then, after changing my nappy one last time, she kissed me goodbye and gave me to a lady who drove me to a home for babies who were waiting for new parents. Before my birth mother went back to Dublin to her job caring for other people, she received a bunch of flowers from her baby's new mum and dad, with a note thanking her for 'giving us Nicholas' and promising to love him and look after him.

And here, as my birth mother left the story, my mum would build up to the happy ending, the bit where I was sort of 'born again'. She would tell me: all the nurses in the home for babies fell in love with you and they held you and they cuddled you as much as they could. And all the other babies kept you company. You were never alone.

When she and my new dad came to see me for the very first time, out of the lots of babies that were waiting in the nursery, in all the cots, in all the towelling nappies, my new mum immediately knew I was hers. She said to the nurse, 'Oh that little sweet baby over there, he's gorgeous. He's smiling at me.' The nurse looked at me and then looked at her. 'That *is* your baby, Mrs Campbell. That's Nicholas, your son.' Then she explained to Mum that babies that young don't smile and I was having wind. But Mum had seen me smile and this, she told me, was proof that me being a part of the Campbell family was 'meant to be'.

When I was taken home, my already-made big sister Fiona was waiting to meet me. Usually in the daytime she was at school but she'd been allowed to take the day off. She was jumping up and down with excitement now that she had a baby brother and that day, as I was carried over the threshold into my new life, everybody's dream was coming true. I was chosen. I was special.

Little boys can grasp subtext. As I got older and understood the gaps between the words – nine days in the boarding house, twelve weeks in the home for babies – and heard my mum's *Jackanory* cadence, this story became ever more mysterious and confusing. Nurses are meant to look after people, especially very caring ones. Why didn't my birth mother have me in the hospital where she worked? Why did she want to get rid of me? Why didn't she want to care for me? What was it about me that she didn't want or like? Why hadn't she fallen in love with me like the nurses who looked after me, who had held me and cuddled me as I lay there without a mother? And how was it, if I was so special, that my birth mother chose not to keep me? The internal combustion that has been blazing all my life was set alight at an early age.

As the Campbell family grew – I wasn't the only new addition – life was happy and secure and if my birth mother could have looked in, she would have seen how much my mum and dad loved me. An animal lover herself, she would have seen how much I loved our other new addition, Candy the piebald fox terrier cross.

The story of Candy felt like part of my own creation myth as our lives were so intertwined. Like me, he was chosen and he was special and he was also the result of a dangerous liaison, when his mother made a wild dash for love. It went like this: one day, when the heat was on, Judy, the fox terrier who belonged to the 'academics' next door, ran on to the main road, dodging the Mini Clubmans and

Ford Cortinas growling along the sleepy streets of south Edinburgh. Her scent was seductive and adventures beckoned. The fact she made it back intact, in one sense at least, was a minor miracle and it soon became clear that a real-life version of *Lady and the Tramp* had played out in the streets of Newington and Grange.

Like all the neighbours Judy's owners were relieved when she came home and then somewhat astonished when she went on to have a litter of adorable white puppies, which, unlike their pedigree mother, were most certainly not Kennel-Club approved.

According to Mum, Dad was famed for saying that his family would have a puppy 'over my dead body', but while the new baby, special and chosen, was being lavished with love, he needed to make his daughter feel special too. Fiona had seen the puppies and of course wanted one, and so he popped next door. And one afternoon in the early summer of 1961, Candy joined the clan.

Dad got the puppy so Fiona wouldn't feel left out, but Candy and I were the same age and the same height and right from the word go, we were on the same level. As a puppy he would sometimes ride in the pram with me when Mum took us for a walk round the block, and we grew up – and down – together. As soon as I could crawl I was crawling with Candy and as soon as I could talk I was barking with him and we were barking at the world. We were the dynamic duo – a six-legged eight-limbed double-act – and he was my brother, my life coach and role model and so I became a real-life wolf boy, the Mowgli of Midlothian, following his lead and following my heart. He made me endlessly happy: an unconditional friend, a wonderfully boisterous playmate. We'd begun our adventure in life together, both of us products of animal passion and happy accident, and we were bonded for life.

When we played together in the garden, I could see Judy through slits in the fence and Candy could smell her. Sometimes we'd bump into her on walks and he was always rapturously excited to see her. But Judy had not the remotest interest in her son. As far as she was concerned he was history and best forgotten, and when I began to understand the nuances of my own story, I decided that people must be like that as well. Like Candy, I too was history and was clearly best forgotten.

Under Candy's tutelage I wouldn't eat anything before first smelling it, a practice that has long outlived those days. Distressingly for my parents, I approached all visitors and strangers who came through the front door on all fours and sniffed them, as did Candy. I sniffed where he sniffed and wherever he sniffed. This pincer movement was embarrassing – depending on the target location of the sniff, occasionally excruciatingly so. We would both be wearily told off in front of the visitors and ordered to get down immediately, as if we were both dogs, which as far as I was concerned we were. Visitors were initially at best dumbfounded by this behaviour, and some must have wondered what it was my parents had actually adopted here, but close friends got used to it and bore it with equanimity. Very early on, as soon as I could toddle and grab, I developed a fondness for dog biscuits – great big deliciously bland, bone-shaped crunchy biscuits, the pauper's digestive. This guilty pleasure has lingered, though I can't stand the rather more pungent little treats you get nowadays. They taste like extreme Marmite.

Our play-fights were epic. Over the years, myriad passers-by would rush up the path to save the little boy who was being mauled by a devil dog on the windowsill. One woman actually hyperventilated while standing at the door. 'For pity's sake,' she rasped as my mother answered the frantic knocking. 'Dog . . .' 'little boy . . .' 'attack . . .'. When she could speak no more, my mum politely thanked her, closed the door and returned to the afternoon radio play, while Candy and I promptly resumed our loving combat.

We were with each other all day and nowhere was out of bounds. When I started going to nursery, Mum told me Candy would go from room to room looking for me, until he laid claim to a chair covered in a tatty old rug in the upstairs front bedroom from which he'd watch the world go by while he waited for me to come home. From then on, as I came down the garden path, I'd look up and see him disappear in a flash as he dashed down for the big greeting, bouncing with excitement onto his hind legs, jumping up to lick my face like he hadn't seen me for years. And then we'd chase each other round the house, up and down our small garden, in and out of the kitchen and down on all fours for one of our play-fights in front of the telly. Over the months and years, the tatty old rug became covered with his white hairs and if ever I needed a warm hug on a cold day, I would lie on it and be calmed.

I was a shy and clingy child and when Candy wasn't around I viewed the world from behind my mum's legs, my thumb firmly planted in my mouth. I was distrustful and even fearful of strangers – unless of course I was sniffing them. And I was sensitive to my beginning, attuned to the precariousness of belonging or not belonging. At the cinema, watching *Dumbo* through plumes of tobacco smoke, slurping my Kia-Ora, I froze in horror when baby Dumbo was tormented by a gang. But then, when his mother rushed to his protection attacking the bullies and *she* was locked in a cage, my panic ratcheted up a level. Dumbo was left with no one to look after him and the force of this made me leap from my seat and run screaming up the aisle, out into the foyer. I was a furious, frightened ball of despair, unable to bear it and unable to watch any more. Like Dumbo's mother, my mum rushed to my rescue and I was safe, but down the long years since, that moment of painful understanding of what it means to be abandoned has haunted, perhaps even tortured me.

Like most adopted children, my identity was fragile and I wished upon wish that I could have been normal and not the child of a stranger. My sister loved me, that much was obvious, tickling me till I was helpless, dangling me over the banisters by my feet, which scared me in a thrilling sort of way. But, as an annoying baby brother, I loved getting my own back. At Christmas, Fiona would count the presents under the tree to make sure she and I had exactly the same number, constantly monitoring the inventory as new presents arrived from aunts and uncles, godparents and friends. I got wise to it, tipping her off that I had more, a provocateur, inflaming her sense of injustice that I, the special one, was somehow automatically worth more. Christmas aside, the zeitgeist was in the air and pretty soon she longed to be an adopted child, often telling her friends that she was, and while I could continue to goad her, I could never tell her what I truly felt: that I'd have swapped with her in return for all the Christmas presents for the rest of my life; in fact, for anything in the world. The roles we take in families can become entrenched and what she never knew and what I could never show her was that, when anyone bandied about the word 'adopted', I'd feel as lost as a child in the supermarket running around looking up and down the aisles for their mother.

I loved my big sister but as our age difference separated us from playing together, I didn't feel rejected or hurt. I had Candy. I'd always had Candy and I didn't really need anyone else. His love came with no baggage – no under-standing of where I was from or how I came to be, no concept of birth children or adopted children. For I soon realised that, no matter how much my family loved me and I loved them, they knew – and they could never unknow – that I was different, that I was 'special'. But Candy didn't care.

As far as I was concerned, Candy understood everything, because he made everything better. He followed me wher-ever I went and I thought of him wherever I was. He was so beautiful; a joyful, playful, affectionate little dog, white, with that distinctive brown piebald face, gorgeous velvety ears and those deep brown eyes full of unconditional and infinite love. And that gaze straight into my eyes. It was like he was trying to work me out and help me; like he wanted me to understand him; like he loved me and got me.

His ears had the loveliest smell I've ever known. Just one whiff of that rich musky aroma and wind against tide became looking-glass sea. I saw myself in a better way. Candy forged me, framing me as a person in ways as profound as my own parents; because as much as anyone he was one of the family that helped create this 'me'. It was a special relationship everybody picked up on, and I loved that they did. He was a huge part of my identity and that sense of safety and confidence he gave me means that when I am with any dog now, the world is a much better place.

When I was eight, my mum, a psychiatric social worker, returned to work. As I got older and eavesdropped on her end-of-day briefings with Dad, Candy and me lying on the carpet watching telly, I heard story after story of children being taken away from their families. On better days, I was sometimes able to hear others too, like the woman who made her husband bathe in Dettol every night, something my dad seemed to have difficulty in quite understanding – '*Dettol*, Sheila? Bloody hell. Are you sure now?' I didn't quite get it either – wasn't Dettol for cleaning germs from unclean *things*? – and on my way to bed I saw a bottle in the bathroom cabinet and took a long deep sniff. I was confused but also clear – if I'd been adopted by someone else, all kinds of things could have happened. I was safe here, with this mum and dad.

At the end of my school day I could just about hold out

– getting the two buses home from the other side of town, passing the old women in their tweed coats and velvet hats on Princes Street, sniffing the yeasty smell of the city's breweries and peaty coal fires – until I could be reunited with Candy, a happy ending to every day. I'd rush up the path, barking my return, grab the key from under a stone on the window ledge and let myself in as Candy flew off his chair to greet me. Ours was an ecstatic reunion.

My parents had a lot of friends; they were sociable, warm and welcoming, interested in people and their stories, and on the weekends, the living room would be buzzing as they talked, laughed, tippled and laughed some more. Before we were shooed up to bed, Candy and I would lie quietly together on the carpet observing and listening through the exquisite fug of pipe and cigar smoke and aroma of McEwans Export and Gordon's Gin.

I stayed on the sidelines. The time had already come when I knew it would not go down well to sniff and bark too much, but I also knew that in order to preserve who I was, I needed to keep my distance from those who knew I wasn't my parents 'real' child. I knew they knew but I wasn't sure they knew I knew and so I was always wary, not wanting to be exposed for not being a true part of this family. I could just about trust myself to trust those nearest to me – Grandpa, my mother's father, who stayed with us for about six months of the year, was my ally. There was nothing chosen about me in his eyes; I wasn't special and I wasn't lucky. I was one of his family, no questions asked, no thought given to how I arrived. I was merely a child to be entertained, which he loved to do. He'd suck his false teeth out of position and make horrifying gurning faces – a dying art – and every time we sat down to eat he'd tell Mum the food was delicious while theatrically turning his face from her view and making an expression of disgust. He did it every time and I laughed every time.

If he knew I was adopted, which he must have, he'd probably forgotten on his way to the bookies. I think he liked me because I gave him something back apart from the priceless reward of laughter. When we walked down the road to the shops – or one time to the slate mine, where he bought me chalk to scratch on a piece of black slate – one hand in his, the other holding Candy's lead, these were moments of complete happiness and safety. I'd ask him about his life and he'd tell me about fighting in the Somme and the football matches he'd seen when he was young. He had the stage, which he relished, and I listened. He never asked me anything about me. Why make an exception? There was nothing special about me.

But outsiders were a different matter and other people were harder to work out, especially when I knew that they knew my secret. Dr Ronnie Cameron was as difficult to work out and as confusing as Grandpa was uncomplicated and while I liked him, I was wary of him too. In my story of how I came to be, my mum's doctor, our family GP, played a heroic role, uniting my birth mother and my parents in their desires. He was part of the social scene and as I got older, I was more aware of his part in my destiny. He was a gentle, caring GP, bald with bushy sideburns and a ruddy pockmarked face. He had an actual fob watch, which he occasionally retrieved for a quick-as-a-flash glance.

He smelt of gin and cigarettes even in the morning and he and Dad made each other laugh – a lot. 'Well done, Nicholas,' he would boom after a chest examination, reaching for a jar on the shelf to reward me for my bravery. But jelly babies were never enough for what I knew he knew. I was Nicky. My birth mother had called me Nicholas and so this was secret code for the cognoscenti.

From time to time, Dr Cameron would flush me out. The Camerons were neighbours, their house on the same road as ours, and I often played with their son Jamie, the two of us tummy-down on the upstairs hall landing, absorbed in the endless manoeuvring of his toy soldiers. During one particularly tricky skirmish, I was reluctant to leave my post and despite two more rallying cries to 'come down', I stayed where I was. Nothing too terrible in this; but Dr Cameron decided otherwise. He stormed up the stairs, his face red, hurled himself at me and dragged me down the stairs, depositing me at the front door. 'There,' he said to my star-tled parents, 'you are too soft on Nicholas.' He knew I was not who I said I was and I felt my shame deeply.

The growing awareness of what it meant to be adopted, to both be a part of and apart from the family, became a tangled path that became trickier to navigate. A misheard word or sentence could set me off and flood me with cold feelings of worry and insecurity. One summer afternoon, as my mum dropped me off to play with some other chil-dren, I overheard one of them talking to her friend. 'You know,' she said in that conspiratorial way of confidences, 'that she's not his *real* mum, don't you?' The rest of that day went on for a hundred years. At nine years old, talking about what had happened with my parents or sister would have made it worse because I just wanted to pretend it hadn't happened. On the way home I cried and Mum said I was tired and that was what I wanted to believe. When I got home Candy, as ever, took me out of myself and into a better place.

From then I was on alert. If my friends looked at me in what I deemed to be a certain way, I imagined they were in on the awful secret of who I was, or wasn't. Did they pity me? Did they think that because my 'real' mother gave me away I was in some way not a real Campbell? That I didn't deserve this life or that I was an imposter in it? And as these thoughts grew louder, there were times when the noise was too much.

My tenth birthday coincided with an Easter break in the Highlands. For a peppercorn rent, from a purple-faced farmer, my parents rented a ramshackle two-roomed cottage that we stayed in two or three times a year. There was no water, no electricity, and the loo was outside, which meant even more exposure to the midges, but it was wonderful and I loved it there, playing in our 'fern village' and splashing in and out of streams with Fiona, who would abandon all of her grown-upness as we ran ourselves to blissful exhaustion.

On this 'special occasion for a special boy', we sat with best behaviour and due decorum in a fancy restaurant on the top floor of one of the big stores in Inverness. The level of luxury was several notches up from our dilapidated Highlands dwelling – pristine white tablecloths, an alcove on fawn leather seating all to ourselves. Everyone was happy in our happy family and it was my actual birthday – the very day I was born.

What a good day it had been so far, with ten-bob notes tumbling from my birthday cards like the fruit in the pub's slot machines. Dad was beaming. 'Well, Nick, how does it feel to be in double figures?' I didn't immediately know what he meant, but as he explained I could sense this wasn't just any old birthday but a special day for the whole family. We were treating ourselves to the traditional four o'clock Scottish High Tea: plates of ham sandwiches, with the option of Colman's English Mustard to bring them alive; scones with jam; chocolate biscuits; pots of tea and bottles of Coca-Cola. I drank mine quickly, bubbling up the last little bit and then sucking it dry, relishing the noise as much as the taste. I held up the bottle to my eyes, lost in the glass contours, and I saw a man tucked away at an organ in the far corner. He was in a black jacket and white shirt, with sideburns like Elvis Presley.

As I blew onto the bottle rim to make my own music, I felt a hand on my arm and I came out of my trance, sensing a flurry of activity. The tempo ramped up and a waiter was standing in front of me, holding a cake with the pomp and pride of the master of the crown jewels. Mum, Dad, Fiona, the cake carrier, the waitress, the rock and roll organ man in the corner, were smiling at me. It was as if I was submerged in a great depth of water. I could feel the vibrations of 'Happy Birthday' and I could see a room full of open mouths but all I could hear was a great whoosh of hailstones crashing around inside me.

I was desperate. I burst into tears. All this kindness and all this love and all this happiness about me. I didn't deserve it. An unbearable sadness erupted. All the wonderful love of the people who loved me was suffocating me and I couldn't navigate the dizzy bewilderment of having arrived at these 'double figures'. Nothing felt real and I knew, in a moment of great clarity that has never left me for a moment since, what it was like to be the imposter. How could anyone be celebrating my birthday? My birth day. The day on which my mum and dad had not even known who I was, the day on which the mother who had given birth to me had already decided she didn't want me. I was the biggest fake of all.

And I was angry and confused that I was angry. How could I be angry with my parents or my sister, their love etched all over their concern for my tears? How could I be angry with my birth mother, the heroic nurse who had given me up for the greater good of others? So I turned my anger on myself – for spoiling this day for everyone – and as I dug my fingers into my fists, I pushed this new feeling down into myself.

I needed Candy. But Candy was two hundred miles south in a kennel in Edinburgh as my father did not allow him to come with us, claiming he was too troublesome, chasing sheep and making a nuisance of himself. I vowed that I would spend the next year persuading my father that Candy should come with us for my next birthday, so I would be ready to celebrate the next year of my 'double figures'.

Mum, Dad, Fiona and me on a summer holiday in the Highlands, 1967

CHAPTER TWO

The Empty Chair

A YEAR LATER and my twelve months of pleading had got me nowhere. Candy remained condemned to incarceration for the four weeks we were away, a prisoner while we ran free.

As it turned out, that was the last summer we left Candy in the kennels. After less dramatic Highland teas, we returned to Edinburgh on a Sunday evening, too late to collect him. Dad said he would fetch him at lunchtime the next day, which coincided with my first day back at school. The moment the bell went, I was out of that playground, racing home, leaping off the open-decked bus and bombing back down the road to our front door. My heart was pounding for Candy, aching to get back into our own little world. Four weeks may not have been double figures, but every moment without Candy stretched to infinity.

As I opened the front door, there was a silence, a stillness I couldn't quite make out. Through the hall's darkness, I could see Mum, standing on the landing.

'Where's Candy?' I asked.

Somebody flicks a switch and everything is different. Nothing Mum went on to tell me made sense and yet her words were crystal clear. Candy was dead. When Dad had arrived at the kennels on that Monday morning, he was handed a very sick Candy. He'd taken him straight to the vet, who told Dad that it would be kinder to put him out of his misery 'there and then'. Dad decided, there and then, to follow 'professional advice'.

The despair that hit me was, and is still, like nothing else I've ever known. Candy was never coming home. I was never going to see him again. I couldn't breathe and I couldn't hear. I ran past Mum, up the stairs to his chair, and I sat on it, inhaling the tatty old rug. I'd never even considered the possibility that Candy would die. He had always been there and always would be.

After a while, Mum came in and perched on the radiator by Candy's chair. She asked me if she could tell me a story. There was a little girl, she said, who arrived home from school and rushed into the house, overjoyed that she was going to see her little dog Tozer again. But as she searched for him, calling his name, he didn't come and she asked her parents where he was. 'Ah. We forgot to tell you,' said her mother, 'Tozer was run over by a car and was killed. Instantly.' The little girl was devastated. Tozer meant the world to her and the thought that she'd not been there to save him, that she was never going to see him again, was the saddest moment of her life.

Mum paused and I looked up. She was sadder than I'd ever seen her before. She reached over and took my hand and told me that I would be sad for a while yet, but I would soon remember what a wonderful dog Candy was and how happy his life had been with me as his best friend.

Later, as I tried to take some control of my grief, I collected some hairs from his chair and tied them together with a strand of blue wool. I wanted to keep his beautiful smell for ever – like some religious reliquary. I also became fixated on placing a notice of Candy's death in *The Scotsman*. I scoured the pages to find appropriate wording and wrote his obituary, careful not to use too many words.

Candy Campbell. Dearly beloved dog and brother of Nicholas. Put to sleep after a short illness and now at peace and always in my heart. I will never forget him because he was kind, loving and beautiful. I will love him for ever.

Despite my pleadings and totally rational argument that obituaries were there to commemorate loved ones and Candy was a *very very* loved one, my parents were not amenable to sharing the news of Candy's death with the rest of Scotland. But they were loving and understanding and there for me and my mum took time and care to reassure me how normal it was to feel like I did. She told me it showed what a sensitive boy I was and that it was good to cry, to not bottle things up, a lesson in life.

For ages after, I felt as if I were dragging my heavy heart everywhere I went. Every time I walked into the upstairs front room I felt Candy's presence. I dreamt he was still jumping up to lick me but I just ignored him or turned my back on him. I woke up crushed by thoughts of his last moments, when he would have looked for me and I wasn't there.

Shortly after Candy died I discovered a story – one that was to be hugely significant in my life and which at the time seemed to be an uncanny reflection of it. This tale was set in the Highlands and it portrayed a unique and magical bond between human and animal that, as was the case in my own life, was cut short by death.

In a bizarre departure from the normal run of the school day, out of the blue or the Edinburgh grey, we were treated one afternoon to an assembly hall viewing of the film *Ring of Bright Water,* based on the book of the same name, a million-copy seller from 1960. It was written by Gavin Maxwell, and in it he described his life in a remote lighthouse-keeper's cottage in the Western Highlands of Scotland with Mij, an Iraqi marsh otter he'd acquired on his travels in the marshes of southern Iraq.

I've always wondered what lay behind that choice of film. Maybe the Edinburgh Academy Preparatory School staff wanted to put some starch in our upper lips, or maybe they were merely hoping to inspire us to explore the book, a Scottish classic, which very soon would appear on the syllabus. It was often hard to understand the motives of the teachers at my school. They were a mixed crew: deeply damaged war veterans unaware of the toll on their minds, relics of Victoriana with mortar boards, elbow patches and half-moon glasses, and some younger go-ahead teachers, one of whom dressed and looked like she should be dancing on *Top of the Pops* to Ziggy Stardust and the Spiders from Mars. Let all the children boogie. Our staffroom represented the dark past and the bright future as the new decade lit up Britain – power cuts notwithstanding.

It was all hands on deck as we cleared away the lunch tables in the main hall, piled them up and hauled them out. We lined the chairs up into an ad hoc cinema and, amidst the clatter, found ourselves seats. We waited; expectant eleven-year-olds not quite sure what was happening but nonetheless excited at the unexpected turn of events. The main hall blinds were hooked and pulled closed, as the huge projector started whirring and the magic lantern's dusty beams banished a humdrum afternoon.

From the evocative theme tune, the opening titles' jerky projector blotches and the muffled booming sound, I was captivated. As the Highlands were such a central part of my existence, I could smell the heather, the bog myrtle, the ferns, wind, sheet rain and occasionally scorching sun. The Gavin Maxwell character is called Graham Merrill in the movie and his craving for the escapism of the Highlands, never mind his special bond with his animal companion, drew me in like nothing I had ever seen before.

As I found out after reading the book later, the film's plot bears a passing resemblance to Gavin Maxwell's original story. Graham Merrill – played by Bill Travers – realises he is just a number, a piece of data, trapped; a wage slave in an impersonal world controlled by faceless civil servants reducing us all to stats on a spreadsheet; rats in a maze. He needs to get out. Wandering through the heart of the city, he notices an otter in a pet shop window, a prisoner like himself, and they become mutually intrigued and on a whim, he rescues this animal before rescuing himself and taking Mij to his dilapidated cottage on the remote Western Highland seaboard.

Graham has room to breathe, think, write and to love his sentient friend, while Mij has the freedom to be an otter, gliding through the wild waters with undulating grace. Graham spends hours sketching his enchanting but mischievous soulmate as the two of them flourish and forge that unbreakable bond of trust between human and animal that can only be experienced to be understood. And I completely understood. I was transfixed. Like Candy and me, they were uncannily in tune with each other and when Graham looked at Mij, I understood that magical feeling of wonder.

The two of them are together through the glorious days and nights save for Mij's increasingly ambitious adventures in the clear free waters of the sea lochs. After he sustains a minor injury Graham goes to the village to see the local doctor – played by Virginia McKenna, Bill Travers' real-life wife – and is somewhat surprised to find that the doctor is a woman. They become firm friends but without the merest suggestion of anything more. This little family classic was as pristine as the waters of the sea loch – apart from, of course, the violence.

Graham has to journey south on a business trip for a few days and the doctor keeps an eye on the expansively intrepid Mij, who one day has an adventure too far and ends up four miles down the loch in the village. Big John, the road mender doesn't see an incomparably beautiful aquatic creature wriggling in his ditch. He sees vermin. The camera looks upwards at the evil face, contorted in psychotic rage, as the murderer takes a massive spade to Mij's head, crushing his skull. Dead. Not even sleeping.

On his return from the Big Smoke to the clean air, Graham

hops on the local country bus home, which winds its way along the tortuous lochside road to his stop. He can barely wait to see his beloved companion and leaps off the boarding step like a schoolboy. My own story was playing out before me. Dr MacKenzie is waiting for him just like my mother was waiting for me. Where's Mij? asks Graham. The doctor's face says it all.

This, the worst scene from my life, was being replayed on a big screen. I began to sob; and I wasn't the only one – there was a collective snuffling from boys all around the hall. We may have been full of bluster around school, but there in that cinema-hall, they had broken us. And because I so understood that unbreakable bond of trust between man and animal, I felt as if I'd been shattered into little pieces and ground into a roadside ditch.

In the coming days, weeks, months, years, I thought constantly about Mij and Gavin Maxwell, and more than anything, wanted to be that rescuing heroic boy who could bring Mij – and Candy and Tozer – back to life. From the moment that film finished, I was on rescue red alert for any animal. And it wasn't just that. I also couldn't stop thinking about cruelty to animals – Mij's brutal murder replaying over and over again in my mind – and I inter-nalised it until it physically hurt.

While we were in the Highlands, animals and nature consumed my imagination. I embarked on a mission to read every single word Gavin Maxwell had ever written and dreamt of a life like his, of having an animal friend like Mij. I sat in the new sun lounge of our cottage, which had been built for a bargain by Frankie Gibson, a charming scoundrel Dad had befriended in the pub. Over pints, Frankie had promised an amazing deal, which ended up being a leaking roof, dripping walls and mildew everywhere, always; but my spirits weren't dampened. I was submerged in magic and when the sun shone on those hills and the lochs sparkled with ring upon ring of bright water, I felt alive. This was a lost world of birds, bees, butterflies and another animal – the Loch Ness Monster – that was to steal my heart and become my walking, talking quest to rescue and protect.

Nessie. I needed to rescue her from death and protect her from a fate far worse than death. It soon became my duty to convince the world the Loch Ness Monster existed and as my obsession grew, so did a dull pain in my heart – a cold panic that we needed to do something before it was too late and the final creature perished. Once that happened, our chance of finding this unclassified wonder of the natural world was gone for ever. But while there was still time, I knew we had to fight because I knew she was there.

To me and a whole host of believers, the evidence was clear – echo-soundings that might not be shoals of fish, grainy photos dating right back to the thirties and eyewitness accounts of striking consistency. And my aunts. Aunt Ethel and Aunt Beatrice, Dad's identical bird-like twin sisters, who dressed the same, smoked the same, lived together and who I adored. They had seen it and they were the twin citadels of my implacable certainty.

They had spotted the 'Monster' not once, but twice. On one occasion they were on a crowded bus and didn't dare say anything lest the driver got overexcited and plummeted from the perilous lochside road into the depths below. With the synchronicity of identical twins with identical coats and identical pockets of cigarettes, their identical plan was to look straight ahead and keep their own counsel. They knew what they'd seen, how they were feeling.

The second time, they were on the shores of the loch on a sunny summer morning enjoying the medieval wonders of Urquhart Castle when a massive hump of around thirty feet swooshed out of the millpond calm, like a whale from the ocean. But this was no whale. While the others around them screamed with the thrill, the twins savoured the strange excitement of the moment, which, less than thirty seconds later, as the hump disappeared and the wash lapped onto the stony foreshore, was over. The sightseers rubbed their eyes. Ethel and Beatrice lit their latest cigarettes and wandered back up the hill in search of two very large sherries. They caught the next bus back along the tortuous route to Inverness in pre-emptive silence, should the hump rise again.

Never to their dying days, which tragically for twins were years apart from each other, did they alter their story, and by then I was in my late twenties, long after apostasy, so I knew these weren't just myths for a thirteen-year-old nephew.

My belief was unshakeable and Ethel and Beatrice's sightings of the plesiosaur were my Visions of Fatima – confirmation and affirmation of my unassailable faith. As we drove along the side of Loch Ness, I would peer intently at the extraordinary 24-mile-long, mile-wide stretch of mystery, face glued to the car window, scanning every inch of the dark water that whizzed past me between the trees that were deliberately conspiring to block my view. Occasionally Dad would drive me the seven miles from the cottage and leave me for an hour or so by the banks with some mini-binoculars, but never the cine camera. 'It'll get wet,' said Mum with a finality that invited no pleading on my part.

We were often on the loch, my eyes on stalks. Out fishing with the chief ghillie of the loch, in return for a bottle of whisky and post-expedition rump steak and rolls, I had my chance. He was on the water all the time and miraculously, I had been allowed on board as he and Dad dipped their whiskies into the loch for a drop of water to open up the flavour.

'Have you ever seen the monster?' I asked.

He looked down at me like he'd just noticed I was there.

'There is no monster.' The certainty in his voice gutted me like a trout in a bucket. But then a lifeline. 'I've seen something six times,' he added, 'but it's not a monster.'

I wasn't going to let that one go.

'What was it?'

'I. Don't. Know.' He said it with the beat of the slowest waltz ever.

He checked the line, sniffed the wind, turned to Dad and they resumed their previous conversation about nothing whatsoever. I stared into the water. Never in my life had I heard such wisdom.

As with Gavin Maxwell's books, I got hold of everything that was ever published on the 'Loch Ness phenomenon' – a catch-all term for believers and heretics alike – and I became furious and all churned up inside when people dared dismiss the incontrovertible evidence. I'd had testimony from real-life witnesses – my trustworthy aunts and the man in charge of the whole of fishing on the loch. I was fired up with it, a seething scorn for the arrogant scientific establishment who refused to invest in a proper investigation. I couldn't understand why not. They were clearly afraid they would discover an extant sea reptile alive at the time of the dinosaurs – and that would shatter their cosy scientific consensus. They didn't have the guts to face the truth.

I wrote all my own thoughts in a book with diagrams and analyses of photos and sundry sightings, fully intending to send my dossier to the relevant authorities. These weren't just the fantasies of a teenage conspiracy theorist.

In the late sixties and early seventies, serious people took this deadly seriously. The dark brooding atmosphere of the loch in that majestic setting, along with the Highland folklore of that mythical water-horse, the kelpie, gave the phenomenon a deeper, otherworldly dimension. Plausible figures were on the case: sensible journalists – measured rational writers – at least one MP and a world-renowned naturalist, Sir Peter Scott. Even David Attenborough refused to completely dismiss the possibility of the monster championed by his old friend Peter. The whole idea set hearts pulsating. This was wild adventure on a new frontier of zoology, on everybody's doorstep – and just a few hours from London.

Some believers wanted it so badly to be true because proving this reality offered a Gavin-Maxwell-like escape from actual reality. They were seeking something beyond themselves and their lives. Nessie was part of a countercultural kickback against the tediously normal. She appealed to romantic iconoclasts, wishful thinkers and, naturally, chancers from far and near.

I heard adults who lived in the area matter-of-factly say they'd 'seen something'. There was Alex, the proprietor of the Glen Urquhart Lodge Hotel and restaurant, who obviously had a stake in the plesiosaur, and Isabel, Queen-of-the-scene in the garage shop and cafe, glamorous, chain-smoking, Rive-Gauche-reeking, who regaled her audiences and anyone filling up with petrol with tales of a late summer's night and a hump. There it was. And there was the author and thespian Clem Skelton, who rode on a wave of relatively successful fiction and claimed to be friendly with 'Larry' Olivier. He flicked the great man's name about like cigarette ash, which my parents found tiresome. In fact, they began to even doubt the connection, complaining that he protested too 'bloody' much about 'dear' Larry. But Clem did have a bewitching fireside delivery for his tales of Nessie. He would intone in the flickering light, with Olivier delivery, the predictable 'there are more things in heaven and earth . . .' because Clem cleaved to the theory that it wasn't an actual animal in there but an apparition – a spirit being. It was a kelpie. Of course it was. He'd become heavily involved with the Loch Ness Investigation Bureau, but possibly never mentioned this to the earnest young men and women with long hair and horn rimmed spectacles fighting like hell for proof of plesiosaur credibility and scientific attention. I liked to think of my new hero the ghillie, not likely a huge fan of thespians, Larry included, chucking Clem Skelton over the side of his boat.

Some local characters were less plausible but 'benefit of the doubt' was doled out in abundance. Two fabulous, dubious eccentrics, Basil and Fatima Carey, elderly expat colonials, came in from the Raj and took to the Glen like fish to water while drinking like a couple too. They made the word 'fuck' sound poetic and quite casually, albeit slur-ringly, spoke of seeing the 'farrr-king monster' on a large number of occasions – every time they went out basically, and I'm pretty sure they claimed to have once witnessed it crossing the road. It was pink elephants and pink plesiosaurs all day long.

I had complete faith in Nessie's existence and I was evangelical in my fervour. Like son, like father: Dad wasn't averse to a bit of proselytising and persuaded the map publishers he worked for to produce 'The Facts about the Loch Ness Monster', a themed wall-chart on which various 'facts', photos, info and an artist's impression of a plesiosaur crowded around a map of the loch, which shone as the centrepiece, complete with a range of thrillingly colourful blue contours. It was all for me.

Then came what I really thought at the time was the greatest day in my life, the 'watershed' moment when I was convinced the world would sit up and take notice. This was all thanks to Robert – Bob – Rines, an American lawyer and inventor who looked like a Democrat senator or former astronaut. He had caught the Nessie fever after seeing a dark hump on the loch one evening while taking tea on its banks and, like the aunts, was in absolutely no doubt that

35

this was an animal. Not a ghost – or a monster – an actual animal.

An interest became a passion, which became a driving, all-consuming obsession for the rest of his days. He obtained sophisticated underwater cameras and, in conjunction with an underwater Edgerton strobe flash camera, there was immediate success – the best of these grainy images came to be known as the Rines/Edgerton flipper photograph and resembles the limb of a plesiosaur. When this was released it was, for me, as big as the moon landings a few years earlier.

This was it. The flipper had been photographed in the dark brown waters and then scientifically enhanced with 'applied science' to show what it really was: the rhomboid swimming limb of a plesiosaurus, a creature dating from the late Triassic age. I practically self-combusted with excitement. How much greater was this than any man coming back from two thousand years ago? How much more wondrous was this than the short hop of a mere rocket trip to the moon? I could see the images there on the pages of my parents' *Daily Express* – a living fossil, from seventy million years ago, existing right here, right now, during my time on earth. And I had a ringside seat, every holiday.

For the next three years Nessie fever went crazy. The monster fed the press and the press fed the monster – or not the monster, the plesiosaur. Charlatans and fantasists aplenty beat a path to the lochside, including Frank Searle, a man reminiscent of the spiv Flash Harry in the *St Trinian's* films, a former soldier who set up lochside, taking and flogging photos of tyres and toy submarines to gullible tourists. He advertised – successfully – for 'Girl Fridays' to share his dream, and sleeping bag, and had a confrontation with Dad at Donny Cameron's garage when he jumped the queue for the till. On the way back to the cottage I heard Dad mutter 'SSC, such an SSC' under his breath, an expression I'd only heard a couple of times. SS stood for self-satisfied, the C was a mystery.

But during the gold rush there were good people too, and before long one of the most distinguished naturalists of the age came searching for treasure. Sir Peter Scott – ornithologist, artist, aviculturalist, conservationist, naval officer, writer, exceptional sportsman, Knight of the Realm – teamed up with Rines. Scott and Rines, my Woodward and Bernstein.

They dedicated every fibre of their beings to uncovering the truth. By 1975 there were more underwater photographs and the cumulative evidence was published in the journal *Nature*. They didn't knowingly undersell. I spread the paper out on the kitchen table and saw things more bewitchingly beautiful and definitively real than I could ever have imagined. Weasels contended that these murky pictures had been polished into subjective clarity, both wishful thinking and enhancement, or declared they were 'tree trunks', but all I could see was everything I'd ever dreamt of, as if it were in an crystal-clear aquarium. Along with the Rines/ Edgerton Flipper photo from 1972, this latest cache made for an open-and-shut case.

With suitable gravitas Sir Peter Scott named the creature Nessiteras rhombopteryx. Taxonomical classification meant species protection and there was no species protection without zoological classification. Ethel and Beatrice were as excited by all this as I was and we kept each other in touch with every twist and turn.

Then something awful happened. A little boy shouted at the Emperor. Someone unleashed the toe-curling anagram of Nessiteras rhombopteryx – a monster hoax by Sir Peter S. – and the whole world laughed. A man of abundant gifts but gentle dreams became, for too many people, a laughing stock. The schoolyard bullies were spitting ridicule; their braying laughter left him numb. Sir Peter died in 1989. Obituaries properly detailed his extraordinary achievements – and all were caveated by that most lethal little word, 'but'. The monster, in the most generous view, enhanced his eccentric childlike wonder. But sometimes mysteries are better unsolved, because it's the mystique that sustains the imagination. Years later, I thought that of another mystery.

Rines and Scott weren't frauds. They were dreamers looking for that something beyond themselves – beyond all of us – but which actually existed; a hybrid of the real and unreal. There's nothing wrong with that and these brilliant men will always be heroes to me, 'but' other scientists, with no agenda bar facts and logic, forensically dismantled our dream. When all that's left is a supernatural explanation, the game's up and this was the beginning of the long slow puncturing of my certainty.

But as the scales fell from my eyes and I could see that the scientific establishment had a point, I remained fasci-nated by the faithful. These grown-ups – adventurers, naturalists and scientists – were children, just like me. Like all of us. And regardless of all the evidence to the contrary – the biological impossibility of a self-sustaining breeding

colony; the lack of physical evidence; the alternative explanations – they still needed to believe the myth, like
playthings of an eternal being.

The Nessie fever subsided and a new generation of scientists moved in to analyse the flora and fauna and
extraordinary geology of the loch. They had no monster in
their view – just clear-sighted investigative realism. While
my dream was terminal, some deep desire for it to be true
remained; and I don't just mean the books, my dossier, the
map, the certainty and excitement of my aunts and the
grown-ups' stories of sinewy humps in broad daylight.

I still cherish the feeling I had. When we are passing by
the loch, as we frequently do on our way to the Western
Highlands, I have to look. Any boat wash, a wake, a ripple,
a swell and it hasn't completely gone, but now I know I'm
not looking for the monster. I'm looking for the boy who
looked for him and wanted to save him because somewhere
he too needed to be saved. It's still me. I'm still there.

One summer's evening, three years or so after Flipper-gate,
my parents took me to a Glen Urquhart drinks party in a
swanky 1970s-modern house, high on a hill overlooking the
loch. The view was breathtaking and, looking down into
the shimmering waters from the grand design of glass and
pine luxury, I thought of Nessie. The house belonged to a
friend of my parents – a local businessman called Gordon
who was openly gay and had a younger boyfriend also
called Gordon, who cut a devilish dash in kilt and open-neck
cotton shirt. Even through my teenage awkwardness, I could
tell that the people in that companionable hubbub of

Gordon's and tonic, Gordon, Gordon and the stunning vistas as the sun dropped in the sky made for an enchanted evening.

As I downed my first Coke, I could hear a man with an American accent, holding a vol-au-vent and court to three or four enthralled guests. I was immediately sure that he was Bob Rines. I watched him for a while, dying to talk to him, but my teenage self was just too self-conscious, so I lurked within earshot as unobtrusively as possible. As the evening wore on and the conversational volume shot up, I could hardly hear what he was saying.

At one point Rines wandered from the throng, away from the cigar smog and towards the floor-to-ceiling window. I was shadowing him like I thought an East German agent would spy, keeping to the edge of the room. As he reached the window, I took up position. He was miles from any other adult now, yards from me, and as he gazed out of the huge window, he stared down the glen at that endless stretch of Bible-black water glowering in the gathering dusk. And then he spoke, his voice gentle, beseeching.

'Where are you?'

High on music, 1978

CHAPTER THREE

Blue-Eyed Boy

BOB RINES' QUESTION had chimed with me beyond the whereabouts of the Loch Ness Monster. I was fourteen and I'd started more and more to ask the same about this mysterious other birth-mother person. What had she been doing all these years? In my mind she had a whole new set of shiny children, getting them ready for school, taking them on holiday, baking them birthday cakes to mark the day she'd had them, never telling them about me, never even thinking about the secret she kept buried. Was she still looking after a lot of other people, in addition to her new children? I was increasingly consumed with a need to know why she had given me away, to understand it beyond the bromide of her being too busy caring for others to have me in her life.

The thought of ever meeting her or any of these new children never occurred to me – they were imaginary people who would never be a part of my real world. Fleetingly, I had constructed my own Brothers-and-Sisters-Grimm forest scene in which I stood gazing into a sort of log cabin where a fire blazed and a mother sat, watching her children play. But in real life I never had fantasies of meeting her properly and getting to know her. She was merely the source of the dull ache of adoption and rejection. Always sensitive to my emotional temperature, Mum could pick up on any spikes or changes, choosing her moments carefully, several times reassuring me about the height and hair colour of my birth mother and birth father, as revealed in the adoption papers. These, she told me with some pride, or relief, were remarkably similar to her and Dad and I came to understand that this nugget was as golden for her as it was for me. I totally got how she needed it to be true and also thought it would help me. Proof indeed that it was all meant to be.

The fact that I wanted to know who my birth mother actually was, and perhaps notionally the anonymous birth father – although he seemed peripheral and even irrelevant – induced a cocktail of shame and guilt in me. Shame that I had been a mistake, something she wanted to wipe out of her life; and guilt that I should even be thinking of wanting to know who she was. The trip to the log cabin in the woods was my secret. Most of the time I wouldn't even tell myself about it. My parents loved me unconditionally and Mum wanted me to be like her and Dad as much as I did. But it started to feel like an ever-decreasing circle: my birth mother had rejected me and now, in just asking the question of who she was, I was in danger of rejecting my parents.

I tried to blend in, to be a Campbell through and through. But I was always scared I'd be found out, and even the most casual or random of encounter put me on alert. One Saturday afternoon, as Dad went to pay for petrol, the attendant leaned into the car to say hello to Mum. Ah, he said, you have children in the back. He peered in closer and in that instant I froze. He was looking and I knew he knew and I knew *exactly* what he was thinking. He had eyebrows like mops and as our eyes met it was as if the world stopped. But instead of asking me for papers, documentation that proved who I was, he smiled. What lovely children you have, he told Mum. You can certainly tell they're brother and sister. I felt so relieved, so happy that I wanted to run around the forecourt, the scorer of the winning goal at Hampden Park. But the moment of euphoria was short-lived, for as soon as we drove away, the sense of cold panic made me feel so lost and lonely in myself that I could barely keep from breaking down into tears.

Occasionally people remarked on how I was 'so like' my dad and I would briefly think: I do belong here completely, this is who I am; and then something would jolt me out of this fleeting sense of security. Often I did the jolting. I wasn't like him – he could make things, had been an outstanding rugby player and loved maps, while I was totally unpractical, couldn't make head nor tail of any map and was a mediocre rugby player. I wouldn't let him come and watch me play because I felt I could never live up to his brilliance on the pitch and it was just too brutal an example of how we were different. He would so loved to have come along every Saturday morning to support me but reluctantly, sadly, he respected my wishes because he never wanted to upset me.

Whenever I wore my kilt I felt this enormous sense of connection to my dad. He was his father's son and I was his, and that meant I got to wear the Campbell kilt. And, as he told me, one day my children would wear this tartan too. I'd got my first kilt aged around five and had always adored wearing it. The fact that of all the clans the Campbells were seen as the most notorious and disreputable added a delicious frisson to wearing it. Like a soldier's regiment or warrior's clan, it told the world in categorical terms where I belonged and who I was. The swishing dash of it all gave me an invisible force field of confidence. I was just the same as everyone else. School events were a kilt-fest as other boys came in their own proud tartans and they could see who I was. I was Clan Campbell, a part of a family, and nothing said one of the family more than a kilt.

Maybe there are some children who take their adoption lightly, perhaps even wearing it as a badge of honour or not giving it another thought. I wasn't one of these. Ever since that terrifying moment of 'otherness' at my tenth-birthday tea, it became a reality that I found hard to dislodge. I lived most of the time without thinking about it but I could be momentarily stunned by the fragility of it all. Who *was* I? I was Nicky Campbell by name but that name and this life that I was living was not the one I had been born to live. It had been given to me by circumstances – a doctor who happened to know a kind and loving man and woman who wanted another child. What would have happened to me if my mum and dad had not known Ronnie Cameron? Who, where, what would I be now?

As the teenage hormones came to the boil and my confusion became noisier, I took it outside myself and aimed it at my parents. I had all sorts of weapons, an abundance of artillery. There was the standard stuff – you can't tell me what to do; I'll come home when I want to come home; that's none of your business. But also: I'm not your real child anyway; I didn't ask to be born; I didn't ask to be adopted; I can't help being a bastard. This nuclear option was mutually assured hurt. I saw the heartbreak in their eyes as they stood face to face with this screaming pizza-faced imposter and I was wounded, but the more they squared up to it, the more I could see it was hitting home and I continued hurling, testing them to the limit.

Through all this my parents never wavered in their love. Mine was as happy and calm a home as you could ever wish for and Fiona and I were thriving. Respecting my 'I-don't-want-to-talk-about-it-but-I-want-you-to-know-I-don't-want-to-talk-about-it' vibe and also knowing what she knew in her professional life, Mum left me pamphlets about tracing and adoption as something I could perhaps address when I was eighteen. My vitriol had clearly hit home but this display was like a scream in a horror film playing out in my bedroom. One glance at the boy on the front of one of the leaflets was like seeing a distorted image of my own face. I felt sick and stuffed them – and part of me – all in a drawer.

We all hold back part of ourselves to a certain extent, but to hold back something so fundamental as my real identity took some doing. On good days, most days, when being one of the family went unexamined, I was barely conscious of it; but on darker days, it took on a sinister quality. Being adopted was a lie I was living and no matter how hard I tried to hide it, it was so central to who I was, that I was not going to be able to hide it.

I couldn't possibly tell my friends I was adopted – that is, that I was a lesser person. They would see me in a completely different light and then so would I. And we didn't sit and talk to each other – the nearest to emotional communication was writing songs with my best friend Robert; we had an unspoken shared sensitivity and mutually acknowledged inner depths – in my friendship group it was, at least outwardly, all about showing off, having a laugh – being boys and strutting our stuff. 'I need to talk to you – I want to tell you something' would have been an extraordinary turn of events and if I had said that to anyone they'd have been expecting some hilarious punchline. Even if I did take someone into my confidence and they didn't judge me, they wouldn't have understood, so nobody was ever going to know. Unless they were clever enough to work it out.

I knew how perceptive Robert was though, as we got each other without saying to each other that we got each other. We had a very different relationship away from the young cocks-of-the-walk, another, double life. Our parents were acquainted and my mum was fond of him. On the way home from school one afternoon, we met up with Mum on Princes Street as she finished shopping. As we loitered around the pick-and-mix in British Home Stores, Robert asked me why my eyes were blue. This is it, I thought, staring at the multicoloured strings of snakes. I willed myself to ignore him. In less than the time it took for him to repeat the question, my mind had raced through a thousand scenarios. The truth could have leaked via my parents to his parents to him, or maybe it was his intuition. Maybe it had always been obvious to him all this time that I was a cuckoo in the nest. Maybe everyone knew, in the same way they immediately would have known that Robert wasn't adopted. He looked like his dad and was also tall; he looked like his mum too and he resembled his sister – not just in height and colouring but because their faces were sibling faces. All four of them had the same eye colour. My family had green eyes. I had blue eyes. Here it was.

Robert persisted. 'Nicky? Why are your eyes blue?' I looked at him, ready to be turned inside out, and he pounced. 'It's because people with blue eyes like us have got less melanin than people with brown eyes. It's a type of pigment.'

I felt dizzy. He was asking me a question because he wanted to impart some new-found knowledge. My insides started to reassemble themselves.

'How do you know?' I asked.

'Learned it in biology today,' he replied. He was in the top set for biology and I wasn't. And with that I was safe.

There was one other secret I was hiding from Robert. Writing our songs, we were pretty confident the world was waiting for our music. What I didn't tell him was that Candy was my secret muse for melancholy – the well of sadness I could dip into for our art and my contribution to one particular 'lost love' torch song.

> *In my life there is no clarity*
> *No faith no love and no reality*
> *Only images of you –*
> *And now you are no longer here – the loneliness is*
>   *getting near to all my images of you.*

I never told Robert what had inspired me but I spoke about Candy a lot because he was there in spirit – we wrote our songs in the upstairs room where his chair had once been; his view of the world. It was impossible staring out the window looking for inspiration without thinking of him doing just that. The only time Robert and I ever had a physical fight was when he made fun of Candy's name – 'a boy dog with a girl's name.' I felt winded and lost it, exploding into a blind rage of flying fists and flailing arms, but my much taller friend was able to fend them off and defuse the situation, realising that he had seriously over-stepped the mark.

Something else as absorbing and distracting as the wonderful solitude of songwriting was radio and I became obsessed – obsessed by the records played, how they were played, the things the DJs said and how they said them. The dynamic was fascinating and seductive, as I the listener was half-eavesdropper, half-participant in an intimate rela-tionship. Some DJs said very little but said everything and others prattled about nothing, but they all created feelings and changed moods. There was a boundless and inexpress-ible magic there. An unreality posing as normality. But what was real? The thought of actually doing that – being a voice on the radio – electrified me. And then – I cracked it.

I discovered how easy it was to get onto local radio phone-ins and, having found that voice, I became hooked. I recruited Robert and our other best friend, Iain, and for months we spent the weekends and school holidays calling up competitions, request shows, music shows and, best of all, news shows pretending to be a load of outlandish characters – pompous idiots, bores, drunks, fools, people with terrible wind, local councillors, old women breaking down hysterically because of neighbourhood vandals, self-confessed vandals bemoaning the lack of 'community centres', concerned citizens, doctors, ranters, know-alls and know-nothings, do-gooders and ne'er-do-wells, people making no sense at all and of course 'experts'. All the tropes, moans and grievances in the air, we smelt and dealt them on the air. Pulling it off so successfully every time gave me a sublime sense of achievement.

I was the best at it, the leader of our pack and I strutted my stuff, recording our appearances and playing them every Monday first break-time, standing room only. I loved the plaudits and recognition, my school friends seeing me in a new light, this subterfuge a million light years away from anything my parents would ever have done. It was totally me, mine.

I was used to holding on to my bad secret. This was a good secret and I found that I needed my parents to hear me. One Sunday afternoon while they were pruning the roses, I had a eureka moment. Sneaking into our small front garden, I placed the radio on the rockery, tuned to the weekly local current affairs programme. Back inside, I sat on the box chair next to the phone, keeping my eyes on them clipping and cutting while I reflex-dialled the studio number. There had been some discussion on the threat of rabies from continental dogs after a ludicrous scare story that they might be turning up in Edinburgh. I was put on hold and, hearing the programme down the phone, my heart cranked up a beat and I was slap-bang ready. As ever, the thrill and adrenalin of live radio was a wondrous thing. I was introduced.

'And while we are on this subject we can actually speak to a veterinary surgeon. Thank you so much for calling us.'

'The least I could do under these serious and very worrying circumstances,' I began, in poshest Edinburgh pomposity, one eye trained on my parents, willing them to listen. 'Rabies is a terrrrrible terrrrrible disease and there is only one certain prevention.'

'And what is that?' asked the host.

'You need to bathe in Dettol. At least twice a week.'

The host, an old journalist with a kindly voice, had no reason to disbelieve me, because I was an 'expert'. 'Your entire body,' I continued. 'Head to toe. Lots of Dettol. It may sting a bit but you'll be as safe as houses. It really is a terrible disease . . .' I could see Mum coming towards the front door and I hurriedly told East Central Scotland I had a horse in the living room to attend to with chronic diarrhoea and I bade them goodbye and good luck. I heard Mum's voice, aimed half to me and half to the world: 'There is a most dreadful man on the radio. Awful. A vet.'

I had to tell her and as I 'confessed' she called Dad and I had to start the story all over again. They loved it, making me do the accent again, and the image of them both, waving their pruning shears as they laughed, is one of the happiest of my adolescence. If they'd picked up the Dettol reference, they never let on. When my friends' parents found out about this 'radio malarkey' they gave them a hard time, cross at their deceptions and hi-jinx, but my parents hid whatever misgivings they might have had – or not had – as their laughter still rang in my ears.

I had my inner world of songwriting and my secret world of radio, the success of which undoubtedly gave me an enhanced social standing that, for a fifteen- or sixteen-year-old developing an interest in girls, was a timely development. A crowd would come round for afternoons and evenings when my parents were out and I would attach the phone to a speaker and entertain everybody, phoning local radio, businesses, local politicians including the National Front parliamentary candidates – numbers all in the book – and meting out glorious justice to those who we thought the most deserving victims of all – the most deeply unpleasant teachers. We made glorious jackasses of them. The boys – and the girls – loved it.

One early evening in the midst of this social merry-go-round, Mum told me she needed to 'have a word'. Now girls had recently entered my friendship group and I was less in and more out of the house, she seemed anxious to pin me down. After supper, I went up to my room and sat on the bed, turning the pages of the *Beatles Songbook*, strumming my way through the best (and easiest) ones until I became aware of Mum's presence on the landing outside. She was loitering, walking from here to there, to her bedroom and then back again. When she knocked and came in, she was clicking her mouth, a sign that something was bothering her. She made her way towards the window where Candy used to sit and watch the world go by and turned to me, leaning against the radiator.

'Nicky,' she said, 'I need to talk to you a little bit about your adoption.' I tensed. This was out of bounds and she well knew it. And anyway, I didn't have time. I was going over to a friend's house and there was a girl I liked . . . 'Nicky,' she persisted. 'Are any of your girlfriends adopted?'

Before I could answer this question, which I assumed she also thought ridiculous, she took a deep breath. 'When your birth mother came to Edinburgh to have you it wasn't the first time she had come here to have a baby.' I stopped strumming, keeping my eyes on the strings.

'Your birth mother came to Edinburgh to have a little girl before you were born and she was adopted and you have a sister somewhere out there and now I need you to be very careful.'

A *sister*? What the hell did this all mean? This phrase 'birth mother' that Mum had used meant someone who was also somewhere out there, but at the same time an unreal person – a notion, brave and selfless, floating in the mist. But now the difference between the unreal and the real was being fleshed out. This was an actual sister actually living among us.

Sisters dangled you over the banisters. Sisters tickled you till you cried and screamed in the dusk as you chased them, holding a spider, through the forest of ferns outside a run-down old cottage. My sister and I sat in the back seat of the Ford Cortina in the darkening car park of a Highland pub sharing Coke, crisps and solidarity as our parents stayed far too long with the locals. My sister annoyed the teenage me so much I crushed a banana in her hair before she went to a party. My sister gave me long hugs and laughed at my antics. Whoever was out there wasn't my *sister*.

I looked over at Mum. She wanted to tell me more. I didn't want to know any more. I needed to close this down so I summoned some humanity and told her I would be careful, starting from tonight. It wasn't enough.

'Do you know any girls older than you?' she persisted. 'Any that may be . . . special?'

That wasn't how it worked. If she had been born eighteen months before me, my 'sister' would be in the last year of school or possibly first year at university. Girls older than me wouldn't be messing around with boys my age.

'No Mum,' I said, 'they're my age or the year below. No danger there.'

My cooperation seemed to signal that we could both be released. At the door, she turned to me. 'Your birth mother, Nicky. It's, er . . . a different father, so it's a half-sister you have.'

She seemed happy with this bit. It made Fiona, my adoptive sister, sound like my real sister and this genetic sister only a half-sister, so not a proper sister at all – just some distant irrelevant relative. As Mum left, I got changed for the evening's gathering. Going 'out there' felt suddenly precarious. I'd be leaving the house with yet another troublesome secret, another legacy of my birth mother, and even though I knew in a million years I wouldn't be asking any girl of any age if she were adopted, the seed of this sister, of what lay behind this 'different father', was planted. As I waited for the 33 to Corstorphine, I started to think about her, who she might be and where she might be, now, tonight, 'out there'. I thought of friends' big sisters, or friends' big brothers' girlfriends, or friends' big brothers' friends' girlfriends. There was a whole network of suddenly potential candidates and she might be lurking in the mix somewhere.

All the girls that night were the same year as me and so there was no danger of her being present. And as I settled into it, her existence became intriguing. I now knew that there was someone not too far away out there, who might understand how I felt. A female version of me, with the same looks, same blue eyes, sense of humour, mischief and love of music, thinking the same things and asking the same questions. What did she know? Pretty soon, she became a hidden treasure, an imaginary conspirator, someone who possibly understood me at the deepest level, who I would be able to talk to about everything to do with this stain of abandonment.

Inevitably too, her existence added to the complexity and emotional labyrinth of the gradually unfolding story, part of a chilling reality as the narrative twisted and the creation myth crumbled. I was now contemplating a joint birth mother, two other fathers and a sister, all in other lives, probably unknown to each other, one of whom was possibly living round the corner. Who knew about who? Who bore any of the five of us in mind? Only the mother this other-mother-sister and I shared had any knowledge of all of us. I was always told she was generous. But since there was another adopted child, she was clearly twice as generous as I'd been led to believe.

The axis of her story began to shift. It appeared she'd made a wearily familiar journey to come and have me in

56

Edinburgh, having already done it eighteen months previously. I'd always been led to believe that a good deal of courage had accompanied her across the Irish Sea, that she was a brave, generous woman making a noble decision. But it would seem that her return was as a result of bad decisions. If the first rejected baby was a sad, perhaps forgivable mistake, I must have been the stupid totally unnecessary one. I was something that should never ever have happened.

And it wasn't only that I now saw her in a new light; I also saw myself differently. Mum had told me as part of my creation myth that, being their longed-for child, I was special. That didn't make any sense now. Second-born and second-hand. Dealing with a one-dimensional birth mother had been much easier to get my head around. In this there was a sense of simple certainty – a clearly drawn character – but these new complications were threatening. Life had been confusing enough without them. So I did what I had to do. I locked her up in a drawer, like the one where I'd stuffed the leaflets, and made myself think no more about her.

Graduation day with Robin and my proud father, 1982

CHAPTER FOUR

It's Getting Hard to be Someone

THE FIRST PERSON I ever told was Morag, a sixteen-year-old femme fatale who blew smoke rings that hung in the air like gymnasts' ribbons. I wanted to give myself to her, and I needed her to love me back. What better than the deepest mystery of myself.

I could only do it from a distance, so I called her one school evening, lying tummy-down on my parents' bed, the extension cord wound tight round my hand.

'Nicky,' she said, and my heart flipped. What if she thought I was a fraud?

'Morag,' I said. 'I need to tell you something secret about me.'

'What?' I heard her shifting to a sitting position on her bed and for a moment the thought of her really there startled me.

'I've never told anyone,' I said, now wild with fear. 'And you can't tell anyone.'

'What?' she said.

'I am adopted.'

'Really?' she said and I thought: she doesn't believe me. 'Where were you adopted from?' she asked and her voice was tender and interested.

'Ireland, I think,' I said, although I knew it was. I liked that she had asked where from and not who from.

'We've got Irish relatives,' she said, a tiny skip of delight in her voice. 'Maybe we're distantly related.'

I laughed, a slightly strangled sound. But distantly related was absolutely fine. I double-locked the intimacy and told her not to tell anyone else and she promised she wouldn't and I believed her and we drifted into chatting about other stuff, until a long, meaningful goodbye, but this one was different. I held the receiver like I was holding her hand, carefully placed it down and maybe for the very first time, I felt like me.

I. Am. Adopted. In my whole life, I had never uttered those words out loud and now that I had and the reaction hadn't cut me into little pieces, I couldn't say them enough. They were unleashed. I was unleashed. 'Hey Jude,' I'd think as I went on to tell one friend after the other. 'Let it out and let it in.' I was now an enigmatic stranger from out of town, seductive man of mystery, rabble-rouser and tortured poet. Heathcliff, Byron, Bowie *and* Lou Reed. I could also play it for laughs. 'You bastard!' someone would say and I'd lunge into hammy Victorian melodrama. 'I was left on a doorstep and my mummy never wanted me. Why are you being so cruel?! *You're* the bastard.'

Embracing adoption as a positive identity was one thing, but even thinking about embarking on any kind of quest was still too terrifying to contemplate. When friends asked if I ever wanted to know my 'real' mother, and the very phrase killed me inside, I'd snap back: why would I want to meet her? She was the one who gave me away. She didn't want me. I don't want her. I did though, from time to time, riff on the sister – a jaw-dropping story because she was out there somewhere in Edinburgh, a seductive mystery that gave my story extra allure. And also because I did vaguely contemplate the possibility of one day meeting her. We had something in common, were on the same side, and that felt safer.

My school encouraged me to make my way in the world, in other words not in their world, and on I went, seventeen, freed from my self-imposed definition-by-adoption – no secrets, new horizons and adequate grades. I went up to a university in a city so different and strange it could have been on the other side of the world. The exhilarating sense of adventure in being there – a combination of the vibrant oil-rich cosmopolis and understated locals with a dialect so unusual it was like learning a new language – made Aberdeen the best place I'd ever been. It was a little Texas and a wee bit Brigadoon and I loved it.

I took up acting and magic mushrooms. Acting was plunging myself into the minds and actions of others. The adrenalin of performing across Scotland with like-minded thrill-seekers and some very talented people was a revelation. As indeed were the tantalising hallucinogenic wonders that covered the parks and playing fields. This was another delicious paradox about an Aberdeen so noted for its dour reserve and bitter chills; there if you looked down hard enough was a mind-zonking summer of love.

Tripping was plunging myself into my own head while also being quite literally out of it. I became fascinated by the extreme experience of hallucinogenic journeys into the centre of the deconstructed mind. The irony of trying to find yourself while actually losing yourself was never totally lost on me but nature's endless bounty beat a pricey night on the beer and through the looking glass was so much more interesting than through the lager glass.

Those nights were a tableau of the bizarre as the mundane became magnificent and the unusual out of this world. A combination of 'Red Star Acid' – making its reportedly heralded return to the city after many a long year's absence – and mushrooms, ungarnished, and time would be Dali-esque, slip-sliding all over the place.

During one trip, in a back room of a tenement flat near the docks, I could see maybe a dozen people in the low-lit gloom, one of whom was almost certainly the brother of a friend of a mutual friend in the same class as someone we knew. A skinny bloke with a cowboy shirt and hair like Carole King was smiling at nothing while rocking back and forth like a guru in an ashram. His girlfriend looked like a tiger. My friend Allan was dancing by himself. I went for a pee, which was a curious experience, and on the way back the banister rail turned into a snake.

As I soaked up the disjointed lines of 'Strawberry Fields Forever', the lava light shapes shifting and the curtains – nothing to get hung about – opening and closing, John Lennon, not long dead, spoke to me. It was getting hard to be someone, anyone, but it was all right and that reassurance was as soothing as the smell of Candy's ears. He said it didn't matter much to him, but all of a juddering sudden in the crystal clarity of that unreality it mattered so much to me. The fact that John said it didn't matter much to him anyway didn't matter much at all. Four in the morning and my brain a carnival of light, I thought about the nurse in Dublin and how she mattered. The world turned in my head and I stumbled out into the night.

I didn't get very far, and slumped onto the steps of another tenement on the waterfront, mesmerised by the street lights reflecting on the sheltered water. I managed to light a cigarette but it tasted like the industrial revolution. Maybe all my life had been leading to this moment, the inevitability of knowing I had to meet my birth mother.

An old man was coming slowly past me, half in silhouette. He shuffled to a halt and looked over. I looked to where he was looking. The oily harbour water shimmered behind him and a massive Norwegian merchant vessel was moored not far away. I could see the lights through the portholes where men were playing cards and writing home. I think the old man was drunk – not completely, but just enough for his purposes.

'Hey son,' he said. He stared at me like he'd travelled the world, maybe on a big ship, and seen too many people all at sea.

I waited for the next bit but got the first bit again.

'Hey son.'

Perhaps I was his son?

'Go down to the beach son. Look at the waves. You'll see a lot of yourself in the waves.'

On he walked with his pocket of pearls. I stayed right where I was. Who else might I see in the waves? Deciding that one day I would find her was an almighty step but acting on it – doing it – carrying it through was different.

Seeing any reflection of who I might actually be, or of her, was for a fantastical future when life would be calm and certain; a time when it had all worked out. Not now. Now was all wrong.

At university I'd already started on Northsound Radio, the local commercial station, actually earning money for doing voiceovers and writing jingles. After graduating and over the next few years, life went into motion blur. Dreams I didn't realise I even had were coming true and before long I was offered the chance to present my own show – a late-night programme once a week for twenty pounds a time, though I thought I should be paying them instead. After getting the job I sauntered out of the building and, once out of sight of the receptionist, production office and accounts department, danced down the road punching the air all the way to the nearest phone box. I dug into my pockets for ten-pence pieces, grabbed the greasy receiver and phoned home. 'That's bloody marvellous,' said Dad. 'Bloody marvellous.' He sounded like he'd be saying it for the rest of the day – every so often, under his breath, out loud, putting down the crossword, laying aside the chamois leather, filling his pipe. 'Bloody marvellous.'

I sent Mum and Dad cassettes of the late-night show every week and they stoically persisted with the Velvet Underground and sundry alien encounters just to hear me talking – or stumbling. It was far harder learning to be me than pretending to be a vet advising on rabies, but I prac-tised and practised, alone in the studio for hours on end, dedicating myself to getting good, and when I was actually promoted to be the presenter of the breakfast show – the primetime slot – they drove up 130 miles from Edinburgh at the crack of dawn to the transmission area, listened, then drove back all the way home again.

My supersonic dream machine was carrying me away, consumed as I was by making my way in radio, which had become the core and focus of my life. I had no time to pinch myself, let alone think; no time to dwell on anything because it was all too dizzying, exhilarating, and my birth mother had nothing to do with any of this.

Within five years I was on Radio 1, via London's Capital Radio, while hardly drawing breath. No time mate. Next amazing thing. Bring it on. I met idols, I was working with legends and I could look down the barrel of the lens and be recognised. People I'd listened to growing up – Alan Freeman, Kenny Everett and John Peel – were colleagues and friends. There were talk shows, debate shows and game shows – the British version of *Wheel of Fortune*, which involved being billeted in a five-star hotel in Glasgow for two full weeks as we churned out four shows a day with not a second to spare. There were Radio 1 Roadshows, voiceovers, offers, *Top of the Pops*, VIP air tickets to interview VIPs, VIP seats at the biggest gigs in town, adventures in Moscow, New York and Bogotá.

Adrenalin was the bewitching drug and fame the dealer. This was the manic normal and guarantor of self-esteem, but I was spinning so many versions of myself to so many different people – including my first wife, who I had married along the way – it was hard to work out which self was being esteemed. Teetering across the high wire, I was plummeting, with no safety net to catch me.

I desperately needed to heal my home life, including my marriage, which had quickly exposed strains and cracks in the relationship and was pretty soon a discordant affair, and since the issue had to be me, surely the reason had to be the overwhelming unresolved question of my life. One night, as I hit the bottom, my wife threw out a suggestion that felt like a life raft. My birth mother could be our last chance and she would help me trace her and in this way, I would know who I was and we would survive. I lay there wondering how it had come to this. Just two hours previously I'd been the urbane master of the microphone, in complete control while jive-talking with the Bee Gees as they chatted about their lives and occasionally grabbed a guitar to strum another song from all our lives, in effortless three-part harmony. But now, away from the red light and my bravado, I had all but deserted myself.

And anyway, I told myself as I got used to the idea, apart from anything, she surely needed to know and had a right to know, dammit. Who wouldn't want to know? If, as I'd imagined back in that Strawberry Fields frenzy, she was a carefree adventurer – a free spirit like Greta Garbo or Katharine Hepburn, living life on her terms, well then of course she would want to meet me. And if, as I had come to perhaps understand somewhere off-script, she wasn't that, I needed to prove her wrong. It's me, I'd tell her. I'm on the telly and I'm on the radio. My face is in magazines and papers. Millions of people know who I am. But you don't. You gave me away and *look what you missed.*

I would be whole. I would be complete. I would be a better me. I would be a better husband. A better son to my steadfast parents, far away from the bright lights of London because I'd be a better person rooted in the inescapable raw truth of who I really was. Mum and Dad were always there for me when I needed them – a quickfire catch-up on life with Mum; a post-match analysis with Dad – but I kept it superficial. I didn't need a conversation about my home life because tactful and sensitive as they were, I knew what they thought. I didn't need any kind of proper conversation.

But I needed one now and, long-distanced from London, called home and, almost as a throwaway, mentioned to Mum that I'd decided to trace my birth mother, and maybe my voice was small when I asked her if she would look out my birth and adoption certificates. If you have a minute, I added, as if I was asking her to find a shirt and it didn't really matter.

I came by the next weekend, running on adrenalin and fatigue from a noisy debate on *Central Weekend Live,* the high-voltage current affairs programme that I presented from Birmingham every week. Dad was withdrawn, quiet, and Mum waited until he'd disappeared into the garden before telling me, gently, lovingly, that she'd left what I'd asked for on my bedside table. I ran upstairs two by two like I'd always done: 2–4–6–8–10 – and up into the room and looked, as I always did, to where Candy's chair used to be by the window. The lunchtime sun was streaming in and with a clarity that took me back to childhood, I imagined he was there, in his special place, looking out over the main road towards Blackford Hill. Watching people and barking at the dogs. I blinked away the tears and sat down on my bed. There by the wall was the old piano that Granny had bequeathed to Fiona in her will and on which Robert and I had written songs to make us world-famous. Just by the bed on the floor was where I played with the wooden fort Dad made for all of my toy soldiers. What was I doing? At that moment, alone in my old bedroom, it felt like a sacrilege that I was doing this here. For the first time since I absolutely decided I had to do this, I got scared of becoming someone else and losing everything.

But I was on a mission and I heard the crack of my wife's sharp words and I couldn't back away now. There was the envelope. As slowly as I could, I pulled out the documents. And, for the first time in my thirty years, I saw her name.

Stella. Her name was Stella. This woman, who had only ever been referred to as my birth mother, had been a concept – a psychological construct and philosophical notion. And yet here she was with a name – a living breathing actual person with a face, eyes, heart and mind, who gave birth to a girl in 1959 and a boy in 1961. Stella Lackey, a woman with an inner life, dreams, thoughts, insights, opinions and regrets. Maybe regrets. This was the brave, independent, altruistic woman who gave birth to her children and took the utmost care to have them adopted into good families in Edinburgh and then carried on with her brave, independent altruistic life safe in the knowledge that they were safe. This was Stella.

There was another name on my birth certificate, that of her baby son, Nicholas. Nicholas Lackey. For a moment I didn't move and felt shards of ice in my heart. I was actually somebody else. There was a picture on the piano of the family at Granny's house and there was me, about six years old, grinning a toothless ear-to-ear grin and proud as a soldier in my Campbell kilt. What the hell did anything mean any more? Was Nicholas Lackey the imposter or was I?

There was another document under the birth and adoption certificates. It was a letter of love from my mum and dad with the story of my adoption – my creation myth. Everything they had told me was there, typed onto one neat sheet of yellowing paper, maybe intended for this moment. As I read it, I realised that Mum had probably been expecting this dreaded – but inevitable – chapter in my adoption story. But, I reminded myself, this wasn't the time to let sentiment get in the way. That's the last thing that Nicholas Lackey would want.

As I left my childhood home, she held me close. 'Whatever happens,' she breathed into my shoulder, 'we've been so lucky to have had you for twenty-nine years, more than we could ever have asked for or dreamt of.' I heard her but didn't really listen. It was just a nice thing to say. What I had in my briefcase was the only thing.

I had the name, so what now? At the speed I was travelling I had no time for time and, as it turned out, I didn't have to wait long. A week later, one of the subjects on *Central Weekend Live* concerned the ethics of the private investigation business. The debate was spiky, the case studies predictable: 'he ruined my life and ripped me off'; 'it was the best five hundred quid I've ever spent' – and a former-cop-turned-PI gave an entertainingly enlightening insight into his world of subterfuge and efficiency.

In the throng of the after-show green room, I saw the broad-shouldered PI chewing a crab claw and glugging a bowl of wine. He had a seventies moustache, greying now, and his gait was large, no doubt shored up by Cadbury Fruit & Nut bars consumed while sitting in cars, waiting and watching. I proceeded in his direction and we traded pleasantries. And out it came.

'I'm adopted,' I told him. 'And I was wondering how easy it is to . . .'

'Trace your real mother, Nick?'

'My birth mother. How easy would that be?'

'Not a problem,' he said as if 'Not a Problem' were a gameshow catchphrase. 'If you have her name and date of birth – not a problem. You got her name?'

'Yes.' Stella, I thought. I'd had her name in my mind all week.

'And date of birth?'

'Yes,' I said.

'We're all names on a computer, Nick,' he said, with tremendous prescience. 'No one is anonymous any more.'

I asked how long it might take to get a contact number.

'Five working days, max, Nick. Not a problem,' he said, and we had a deal.

Over the next few days I felt incredibly alive. Something overwhelming was unfolding, and at such a pace that I knew this was bound to provide the answer, whatever the question was. When this was sorted I'd finally arrive at a better place and live happily ever after. Sure, there might be hiccoughs and sensitivities to overcome if she was married with family or whatever, but there was absolutely no way she – they? – wouldn't want to meet me and see what had become of me. She would realise I was famous, in a way, and wouldn't that, in my current mindset, be the ultimate validation for both of us? She might even be proud to see that her little boy had done well.

Seven days later and I had a message to call the sleuth, who was no sloth.

'I've found her. Sorry about the delay, Nick. Weekend got in the way. Wasn't a problem. Stella lives in Dublin still, but hasn't been at her address for a while. She's been away travelling for some weeks, it would appear.'

Travelling? Yet another giant leap towards her person-ness. As I'd suspected, Stella – intrepid and independent – went away for weeks at a time. A free spirit, hiking in the Rockies of Canada, browsing the art galleries of Italy. Whatever she was doing, I would be her greatest adventure yet.

He gave me her number. I stared at it, a sequence of digits that would crack a code. This was an actual telephone number, with real digits and a proper prefix. She had a phone that would ring and she would hear it and pick up the receiver. And I could actually pick up my phone, dial the number and speak to the person who gave birth to me. Where to begin with what I would say?

I got her number on the Thursday and prepared myself

to phone the next day. But on the next day, I couldn't do it. The more real this all became, the more terrifying. I'd do it soon. Maybe tomorrow. Definitely tomorrow. What if she did actually deny me? 'Who? I don't know what you're talking about,' or 'That's a part of my life I want to forget.' Or worse still: 'I didn't want you then. What makes you think I'd want you now? Never call me again.' I'd be in a kind of hell for the rest of my life.

It was all I thought about day and night and the next morning, after an unsatisfactory gin-tinged sleep, I knew I had to do it that evening. Six o'clock came and the piece of A4 with the number on came off the shelf. I walked from room to room like an estate agent on speed. I had no no-problem bravado now. Never mind looking down a TV lens or into a microphone and saying to millions, I am Nicky. I was going to say I am Nicky to one person and it was the most nerve-racking prospect of my life so far.

The ringing stopped and after an eternity of clunky receiver positioning, I heard a faint 'Hello?' A name, a number and now a voice. My wife asked if she was who we thought, and explained that she wanted to talk about a baby given up for adoption in Edinburgh many years ago.

'Deirdre?' rang out the voice. 'Is that you, Deirdre?'

I leaned in to the receiver.

'My daughter. Deirdre! Is that you?'

I took the phone.

'Stella, it's Nicky here. Nicholas,' I said: 'I hope you don't mind me ringing like this but . . .' 'Nicholas? Nicky?' She sounded flustered, but pleased. 'Oh. Well now. How are you?'

Her voice was friendly, encouraging and I said: 'Fine, thanks. And how are you?' and she said she'd been 'up and down'. I didn't know if she meant for the last three days or the last thirty years. She hadn't been travelling recently, but had been ill and 'recuperating'. Her voice was soft and sounded kind, with a hint of fun somewhere in the middle distance.

I told her I was a TV and radio presenter in the UK, presenting a show called *Wheel of Fortune*, a game show. 'Oh yes.' Her voice lightened. 'Is that you now? I've seen that – it's a good show, right enough.' She seemed amused and surprised, but for this thrilling revelation, I'd been expecting more: oh my God. Christ on a bike – that's *you*? My little primetime baby on primetime TV watched by millions. The wheel of fortune really has spun in my direction.

I asked if everyone knew about 'us'. 'Now, why would I do that?' she said and I heard just a wee bit of grit in the oyster. 'It's not been anyone else's business.' Protecting myself against any rebuff, I asked no more questions. Instead, we agreed to send photos and I asked if she was free in a couple of weekends' time to meet in Dublin, and without hesitation, she was. We'd make arrangements. We'd see each other soon. She said goodbye, and this time, I said it back.

An envelope, addressed to me, arrived three days later. When had my birth mother even written my name before?

I stood in the hallway, and I shuddered. I was about to see the face of the woman who gave birth to me, the first person genetically related to me that I'd ever seen.

There were two photos. One was of two young girls in their school uniform and the other a group of people standing outside the door of a terraced house, and on the back of both she had written which one she was and who everyone else was. I stared and stared, but couldn't see myself at all and really, I was the first and only person I was looking for. In the more recent one, there she was, an old woman in a tweed coat, a round friendly face, smiling beside nephews and nieces. Her sister stood to her left. I couldn't see myself at all in these strangers. I tried to imagine me growing inside her and her picking me up and putting me down. I looked and looked again and something about her seemed far away, as if she were there in a happy group, but her sweet Auntie smile didn't tell the whole story, a story that no one else in the photo had a clue about. I picked up the letter and read through the inventory of her relatives – my relatives. The two schoolgirls were nieces, daughters of her brother John, a 'cycling champion', whom she'd adored and who had died 'suddenly and devastatingly'.

The word 'Uncle' took on a whole new meaning. I used to call some of Dad's friends 'Uncle', and Mum's sister's husband who I played chess with once was 'Uncle' John. But this man, Stella's brother, was a gold-plated diamond-encrusted uncle de luxe, the one I'd never meet. I'd never look in his eyes and wonder if I'd look like that one day. Stella wrote that he was a cycling champion – I'd been good at cross-country. Were the two things related because we were? There were so many things to discover and curiosity was like a caged lion.

It was two more weeks until the Easter weekend. I already had my ticket. I was going to meet the nurse in Dublin, the woman who had given birth to me. Stella. Not a problem.

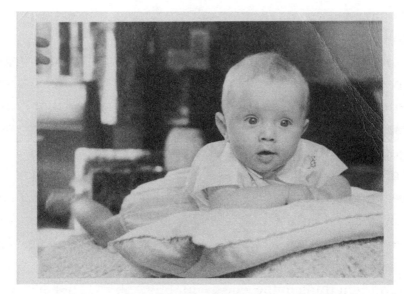

Stella's Long Lost Son, 1961

CHAPTER FIVE

Do You Like Dogs?

THREE WEEKS AFTER first talking to her, there I was in Dublin.

However much I tried to focus on my bravura investigative assignment, the other stuff – the mother stuff – began to envelop me. The notion that this was about flying in, meeting her, getting a bit of background and heading home put me at a useful remove from the terrifying reality. But I'd been kidding myself and when I arrived in her city I began to think properly of what was going to happen. And that was when the panic set in. I was about to meet the woman who gave birth to me. I kept thinking about the 'mother–child bond'. Didn't people say this was the most important thing in the world – for humanity, for our species, for any species – the purest love? Wasn't this where everything began and by which we were emotionally sustained for all of our brief lives? And I was going to feel that sacred bond. For the first time, I began to wonder if this was what I really did want. Didn't I already have all I needed from my mother? I realised this was far bigger than I'd envisaged. There, in a hotel room in Dublin, on the morning I was about to meet my birth mother, thoughts that had never occurred to me were swirling around my head. I was scared, so scared. Scared she was curious and intrigued, nothing more; scared she would care, scared she wouldn't; scared she would break down, sobbing for me; scared I'd be completely underwhelmed and scared I'd be totally consumed by this uncontrollable irresistible force of nature. When it all came down to it, the thought that I might love her was the most terrifying thing of all.

We'd arranged by letter to meet in the reception-restaurant area in a city centre hotel of her choice, at two p.m. It was a Saturday. As I arrived, early, as ready as I'd ever be, I felt calmed, at least a little, by knowing that the wonderfully free spirit who took time out of her life to make sure we were going to be okay would obviously be quite nervous; but she'd no doubt take it all in her stride. The idealised image was lingering. Still I thought she would breeze in – even float through the lobby, bathed in light, dispensing warmth and munificence while all about looked on in wonder at this vision of grace; this iconic mother. A woman so ahead of her time – so fiercely independent, compassionate, caring, loving but defiantly determined to do the right thing.

The initial hello was making me even more anxious. Saying the word, agonising about which syllable to emphasise and what tone to give it. There are a thousand ways to say 'hello'. Maybe I should just say her name. Or both. Hello Stella. But that sounded too staged and deliberate. Possibly even censorious. I had no idea what I'd venture after that. I had an aversion to small talk, but now it might be necessary, to keep it all going. And while any kind of rehearsed speech would be trite and surely transparent, maybe some kind of offer of exculpation and forgiveness was the way to go. I just want to say, Stella, I might say, that I bear you no ill-will. I understand there was nothing else you could have done. But was that patronising? Pompous? I started to think about hello again – which maybe sounded creepy. If nothing else though, I had to tell her that I'd always thought about her and this was a dream come true. I had to tell her that, didn't I? It was the right thing to say, wasn't it?

The more the hour approached the more my script seemed so untrue. I wanted to tell her how amazing my parents were. I wanted to say that Dad was brave, gentle and strong and had fought in the Far East during the war, making the rank of Major, but that in his modest way he never spoke about it. I wanted to tell her that he was always there for me. I thought about telling her how Mum was also a woman ahead of her time, wise and warm; I didn't come from her womb but I came from her heart – her love made me who I am. That she was always there for me. That she always told me how kind and wonderful Stella was, and isn't it amazing, Stella, that my mum said that. I wanted to tell her what my life had been like and how lucky I was to have such incredible parents. But would she take it the wrong way? She might be instantly wounded, cut in half, if I said all that, felled by my jabbing finger, salt rubbed into her wounds before we had a chance to heal them. I had no protocol, no way of knowing how to behave, what I could and couldn't say. Did redemption come at a price?

Maybe I could say it all and she didn't have any right to feel aggrieved, deserved to hear it all. But then, I figured, mums and mothers are different things and telling her about my parents may not even be relevant. And anyway, we were bound to be in a mother–son cocoon, where the world ever since my adoption was a world apart.

With an hour to go before two p.m., this cacophony was blasting through my head, threatening to undo me. I opened the bag of books I'd bought earlier that morning. This was the seventy-fifth anniversary of the Easter Rising and I could at least escape the interminable agony of waiting by immersing myself in the history of my 'people', the tribe I'd been taken from. I'd even bought a scrapbook and a stick of glue for newspaper articles about the commemoration. A scrapbook? I'd last had a scrapbook when I was eleven, filling it with pictures of plesiosaurs and articles on the Loch Ness Monster. And the books. Nine of them. I'd stood looking in the bookshop, choosing book after book, off-the-shelf heritage for a bedside mountain. I'd hulked them to the till like a brickie and only realised just how many when I paid.

But there in the lobby, waiting to meet my maker, I couldn't concentrate and the words swam across the page and anyway the past seemed too far away. I looked around at the place she had chosen for the present, a nondescript entrance hall and staircase up to the reception on one side of a large bright dining and lounge area – more a hall than a room; more a restaurant than a foyer. A couple of years previously I'd been to the Soviet Union to make a programme about the dog days of communism, and looking round now I detected a touch of the same drab half-hearted decor, so at odds with the city dancing outside. The coffee came, aptly, from a large silver samovar in the corner and was served with portions of long-life milk and shortbread, and in spite of the depressing furnishings there was a jolly Saturday-lunchtime hubbub, the mainly elderly customers exchanging scuttlebutt as they savoured some of life's little pleasures.

At 2.30 she still hadn't arrived. I didn't doubt she would show but tried to understand why she might make the decision not to. She was trying to escape; it was too much: too much to expect; too much to live up to. People emerged into the mezzanine area up the flight of stairs but none were her. My mind was a helpless blur of strangers.

I was still all the while obsessing about what I would say, but now I worried about how I would greet her. Put my arms round her? I panicked slightly. I'd never been a hugger, or rather I'd just been a very selective one. Too often it went on a second or three too long. Far better to quickstep forward, medium-strength hold, then step back and retreat back into my personal space. Then I remembered. This encounter may be beyond my control, determined by that instinct far beneath the conscious, so that within a millisecond of seeing her all forebodings and misgivings would vanish as we ran into each other's arms, a magical umbilical bond restored and my need to hold and be held reborn.

It was 2.45. It would be just good to know she was okay and perhaps say a fleeting 'hello goodbye', see a cameo even

81

of the person she was before I became an awkward truth. I'd looked at her photo every day to try to see who I was and who she was, but people don't look like photos. The number of women in their sixties and seventies with tweed or similar coats and glasses, in the seemingly endless parade who walked up the stairs looking around for their own rendezvous, was extraordinary, as if I were in the midst of a convention of former nurses meeting their former babies in a hotel of former glory. That, or an identity parade of birth mothers looking for the baby they'd given away.

I became convinced some of them were her, until they ignored me, looked through me, walked past and walked on. Some glanced at me, clearly wondered why I was staring so intently, and rapidly glanced away. They were probably called Agnes, or Mairead or Coleen. Or even Deirdre. I wondered what my long-lost sister was doing right then. I was taking one for the team – being the bold brave bois-terous brother, jumping first into the sea.

By now so many internal soliloquies were jostling for my attention. She was an hour late. Maybe she had the wrong time or the wrong hotel. I ordered a pint of Guinness to loosen up. It went down in three, the hit of the burnt hoppy aftertaste startling me to my situation. She wasn't going to come, was she? It was either all too much for her, or all too little. Nearly two hours gone and I felt angry, upset, confused, but in a way, at that particular moment I found an alcohol-abetted sense of finality, the last drink in the mezzanine saloon. That was it – not very much at all really, but that was it.

But then, the bitter aftertaste and I felt myself getting

unreasonably tetchy – petty about her tardiness. I was a stickler for timing; punctuality meant a lot to me. It measured a certain *willingness*. By now I'd given up. She wasn't going to show up and I was going to leave. As I looked over to the stairs again and then right, a slightly dishevelled head bobbed into view and a woman emerged, an air of chaos about her. She looked uncertain and fragile. She looked left, then right, all around, and repeated the movements like she'd lost somebody. Then she looked in my direction, without even seeing me, and she walked towards me trying to shake herself out of the panic. She looked frightened. I thought: look what I've done to her. Look Deirdre, look what we've done to her.

I shot up and took a step towards her and I granted a cursory peck on both cheeks and we sat down. I didn't hug her. I'd kissed her, or kind of kissed her, because that's the least thing you can do when you meet your birth mother for the first time since you were nine days old. I guess the most I could have done was a long tight bear hug and then clasped her head into my chest and kissed the side of her head before pulling back to look at her face and doing it all over again as tears of joy cascaded down my cheeks. But that would have been a lie, so the most I could do was the least I could do.

I felt no emotional connection, no spell was cast and the kiss had been as I would kiss an aunt. Not like my real aunts, Ethel and Beatrice, who gave me hankies and ten-bob notes every Christmas. When I kissed my birth mother, I had a feeling like a finger in a socket. If I was a part of her, which is what birth children are, kissing her should

83

have been the most natural easy thing in the world. She had been the first person I touched, but now felt like the last person I wanted to. She was the first person who kissed me and now I had kissed her. I felt numb, nothing.

And she was talking and I couldn't hear what she was saying. I made myself listen, focusing on what seemed to be a frantic, faltering explanation of why she was late. Something about her being so anxious she'd had to take a sleeping pill and had slept right through the alarm. She kept apologising, and then I snapped into action and, as kindly as I could, told her to stop saying sorry and she apologised for saying sorry again.

'Don't worry. You're here now,' I said. I felt like a social worker, not a son, and I wondered why I was here. I didn't know what to feel. I'd come to meet her so that she could make me better and maybe make her feel better, but again I started yearning for my mum and dad with this over-whelming aching sadness and nagging guilt, because I was being so disloyal. But then I switched loyalties in a heartbeat; surely I was being disloyal to my birth mother too by dis-avowing her at this potentially redemptive moment in her life? Loving her like the son I technically was surely should be my side of the bargain and I'd let her down. I'd let everybody down. This was awful.

By now, sixty seconds in, we had travelled far beyond the land of language to a place where there is no place to hide. Where words are a diversion, a regression from truth; there to hide not reveal it.

I folded my arms, hugging myself, for as long as possible. She looked brittle and clung onto her bag like her life depended on it. All our words were just words; dead words. Stillborn.

'This place can get very busy,' I said.

'That's true enough,' she replied. 'It's the Easter weekend and a lot of people come to stay in Dublin. The traffic was terrible but the bus wasn't too bad.'

'How far do you live from the centre?' I asked.

'Not too far now.' She was taking off her coat, here to stay, for the time being.

And as I asked her about which bus and she told me the route she'd come, the extraordinary concept that any of us ever existed in another person's womb played in my mind, always so difficult to grasp, and I couldn't believe I'd once existed in hers, and there she was in a chair opposite me.

We stared and stared at each other, looking for an essence of ourselves in ourselves, but all I saw was an elderly woman trying desperately to cope with an unimaginably difficult situation. Part of me had been expecting a timeless ageless figure who had only just got back to Dublin from Edinburgh, perennial as a character from a children's book, forever young on the page while the rest of us grew up and grew old. I hadn't been expecting a woman in her late sixties because that didn't make any sense at all. In my mind she was frozen in time and I was and always would be an adopted child.

'Oh look,' said Stella, her voice suddenly lighter, 'there's a lovely dog over there.' She pointed to a Labrador, a guide dog, docile and obedient by its owner, and in that moment all I wanted to do was get up, go on all fours and connect with that dog, stroke his neck, tickle his ears and feel that warm rush of reassurance as he looked into my eyes. 'Do you like dogs, Nicky?' She said my name and I shuddered. Nicholas was the name she'd given me, 'my given name', but she'd said 'Nicky'. Did she ever intend for me to be a 'Nicky'? She just had to accept it now.

'Yes I love dogs,' I said and I wanted to tell her about Candy, but by giving her my childhood it would seem like I was making a point: see what you missed. So I kept him out of it and went general. 'I absolutely adore dogs,' I said and she warmed to my response, and that's when I saw her for the first time, a fleeting glimpse of Stella, the vivacious woman of life and legend.

She shifted in her chair and cocked her head to one side, playfully, inquisitively, and as she moved backwards to get a better look at me, like an art connoisseur struck by a deeper meaning, I saw this spark in her eyes, a look that seemed to explain everything. It was self-aware and whimsical. It said, caution to the wind, to hell with them all, it's my life and no one else's. It said, bloody hell, that's him right there and I'm right here in the middle of this astonishing moment. It was an amazed and amused moment relishing, cherishing, for all our woes, the beguiling absurdity of life, with her irrepressible sense of mischief. There aren't too many times in any lifetime that reveal a life in one look. It was a vignette of the brave selfless free spirit of her younger self. I saw her and I saw the person she was and the reason I was. It was her but, then like a will o' the wisp, she was gone.

And as we reverted to nothing-speak for a while, I started to feel the beige walls closing in again, so to break the intensity I sought the loo, a giddy headrush threatening to overwhelm me from getting up too quickly, and from seeing the human being who gave birth to me and gave me away. There was no escaping and the 'restroom' was anything but, merely the same prison, different acoustic. Turning round to wash my hands, I glanced into the mirror and saw that someone else was there. Who was that? It was me, but I didn't look like me any more. I was looking at someone looking at someone else. I slalomed back through the tables and normal service was resumed; the stream of banality flowed into a sea of nothing and we paddled in the shallows, avoiding the waves. The waves? Nothing to see here.

I concentrated. I asked about her love of literature and poetry that she'd mentioned in her letters.

'Were your books a comfort in the . . . difficult times?' I asked. 'After Deirdre and I had . . . gone.'

'I love Yeats,' she replied. 'Do you know "The Wild Swans at Coole"?' But I didn't and swans were not my story. I needed to get to the point. My birth and my adoption. Why else was I there? 'So,' I said, 'tell me what happened.' 'I took a sleeping pill,' she looked sheepish, 'so I'd get a good night sleep, and slept right through the alarm.'

This was one tricky interview.

'No, no,' I said, trying to put her at her ease 'I meant, what were the days like in Portobello? In Edinburgh?'

'Oh,' she said, seemingly relieved I wasn't taking her to task on her punctuality, 'I had good friends in Edinburgh and it wasn't at all a difficult birth. You were a very good baby. And you arrived perfectly on time,' she added and I thought: Punctual. Unlike you.

87

The game of seek and hide continued. I wanted to find stuff out but she just wanted to snuff it out.

'But,' I persisted, 'I mean, it must have been a terrible time for you when I was taken away?'

'Toby was looking for you for a while after you'd gone, right enough. He wasn't at all happy when you left,' she said, as if getting on the wrong side of Toby was a brave thing to do.

'Toby?' Who the fuck was Toby? This could be another shock of Deirdre-like dimensions.

Stella smiled, looking at me directly. 'Ah, he was a lovely little dog, Toby. You like dogs now don't you? You said so? Oh, he was a lovely little dog. He wouldn't leave your side and if anyone came near the cot he'd growl at them. A little growl, like he was saying get away from him now. He used to guard you all day and all night.'

So Toby was a dog; a beautiful dog that loved me. Immediately I felt calm and secure.

I looked at Stella. 'What sort of dog was he?'

'A mongrel. Uncertain parentage as they say. A collie cross.'

And as she spoke, Toby was right there, darting between the two of us with his ears pinned back, wagging his tail and demanding attention and affection. I was rubbing his ribs as he put his front paws on my thighs and I sniffed his ears and kissed his head. Whatever else was happening, whatever sadness and stilted communication there was in the hotel reception foyer, whatever destructive misery there had been in that room in Portobello, Toby was making our world a better place. Dogs make everything better.

'Yes, he would have had some collie in him for sure,' Stella said as if he'd been right there in her mind and she'd had one long judicious look at him like an official at Crufts. And then this bewitching tale unfolded, a bedtime story for a Saturday afternoon. Toby belonged to Stella's friends who ran the boarding house where she took refuge and gave birth. Clearly at such an awful time he was a source of diversion and delight. He took to Stella the moment she arrived, remembering her from her last visit to the city. He was loyal and intelligent and I became the focus of his affection. At his most protective he had a low guttural growl, a warning growl. He even got slightly grumpy with Stella sometimes when she lifted me off the bed to change me.

He refused to leave my side unless he absolutely had to, and when he returned from his walk on the nearby beach he darted straight back in there to get back under my cot and guard me. The way she spoke about him and told me his story, or our story, made her happy. No need to address the despair and misery, only this little dog, this saviour. She was animated and engaged and still delighted by him. He loved me, guarded me, wanted to be with me, and was desolate when I left.

The three of us had shared those nine days and although Stella had the love and support of her friends who ran the lodging, Toby did what special dogs do. He made the world better; more alive. His sentience drew the poison of the wretched situation as he put himself into the emotional triangle of that room, and all his instincts were to protect.

He never let us down, a constant joy in that cold universe of blue.

This was Stella's account of those desperate last days with me and this was our connection. There in that boarding-house room, one little animal on the bed and one underneath it, and although she couldn't protect me, Toby could. Although she wasn't allowed to love me, Toby was. And while she couldn't stand at the window pining and waiting for me to come back, or bark when a well-dressed woman came in a car and took me away, Toby could and Toby did. Toby was there to keep us going, then and now.

'He loved to lick your face,' Stella told me, as Toby ran through my imagination.

'Did you not try and stop him doing that? As a nurse?' I asked, hoping she'd made an exception because I was rooting for Toby.

She was still a giggling student nurse – or whatever time in her life was when she giggled most – and there it was; I saw it again, that sense of devil-may-care mischief that was, by definition, the cause of my existence. I think Toby licking my face had been the least of her problems and thank the gods he had been there for us. Then and now.

The intensity of that afternoon had been overwhelming, but Toby had been there for us yet again. We parted with a brief peck on the cheek before some downtime and then an evening meal at her flat in a sheltered housing complex. Her friend would be accompanying Stella, which I guessed was for moral support. I went back to the hotel, zombie-walked to the room and fell onto the bed, dead inside; a dull ache of nothingness, and feeling nothing, which was the worst pain of all. I had that tummy feeling that isn't the preserve of our own species. It's animal-panic and I was frightened and lost.

I was upset when one mother took ages to turn up, shattered when she did and then poleaxed that my mother or adoptive mother wasn't there to mother me, a childlike feeling I'd last had when I was a child. I curled up on the bed in a foetal position before even realising I was involuntarily enacting an actual cliché of birth trauma. I wanted to be infinitesimally tiny. I needed to be all curled up and safe and I'd never felt like this before, as far as I could remember.

Mum and Dad knew I was here and why I was here. The bathos of meeting my birth mother was devastating, but my heart was breaking for them again. This evening while I was supping with the birth mother who had taken absolutely no part in my life beyond nine days, they'd be there in our cosy front room, staring at the fire, staring at the telly, watching the clock. Did they think they were losing me? I remembered what Mum had said when I came to Edinburgh to get all my adoption papers: 'We've been so lucky to have had you for twenty-nine years, more than we could ever have asked for or dreamt of.' Now, away from the manic mission I was taken over by at the time, I heard her properly and understood her words.

I lay there clinging on to myself, feeling like a traitor in a straightjacket. Not merely disloyal but treacherous, because I'd been threadbare with the details of who Stella really was and what she was doing now. I reckoned it was my business and no one else's and anyway I couldn't be dealing with it in any other way, because if those worlds collided my heart would explode into smithereens.

I closed my eyes. The pain of nothingness was still there, lead weights clamped to my brain. As I started to drift, my mind slipped into the most basic comfort I knew, as Toby became Candy and Candy became Toby. My dogs were there for me, looking out for me, and for two delicious hours I slept like a baby.

At Stella's flat for a reunion dinner of chicken Marengo and warm white German wine, she huffed and clucked around like she was auditioning to be my mother, as if the last thirty years had never happened. But I wasn't looking for a mother. I had one, and as the worst intensity of the afternoon flooded back, I felt myself sinking again and wanted to go home. From the minute I arrived, I was planning my escape. I wanted to run for ever, but this was now it for ever. I was the sad elephant remembering the world he'd been taken from, breaking out of a zoo and running amok in the traffic, tragically thinking there was somewhere to go.

Being a mother or a mum or a mummy wasn't her right. As she pottered, fussed, filled a glass I hadn't touched or asked the same question for the umpteenth time, her friend got it. Leave the poor chap be, Stella, she said. The role of mother is taken, she didn't say.

In the deathly-silent taxi ride back to the hotel, something occurred to me. Not in her letters, nor in the meeting in the hotel or the time in her flat, did she at any stage ask anything whatsoever about my life or upbringing. Not a thing. I excused it. That didn't matter. Maybe any whisper of it was too painful a glimpse into the life and love she'd relinquished, a family picture she daren't look at. That bit was completely understandable – but then wouldn't she want to know just a little bit? For her this seemed to be year zero. A chance to start again – to play a part in the ongoing mothering of this 30-year-long-lost son.

And across the ocean, across the Irish Sea, the end of a long evening was coming to a close. Mum would be re-assuring Dad: Don't fret, Frank, he'll call tomorrow, she'd be saying as they closed up the house for the night, drawing down the blinds and climbing the stairs, one by one. It had been a long evening and they were not done worrying.

Into the night on Radio One, 1992

CHAPTER SIX

Into the Night

WHAT NOW? I'D got what I wanted from the mother-and-child reunion – I'd met her. I'd found out who she was, how she was, where she was and what she was. Maybe even a sense of how she used to be, once upon a time. But for all that I felt empty. And confused. As adopted adults we may think we can understand and rationalise this journey home, but there is something about meeting a birth mother that is so entwined in the mystery of existence it is an experience beyond our normal reality. You're a child again, so how on earth can you understand? Or fend for yourself?

As far as my mum and dad were concerned, and they no doubt were, I was bound to call them the next day to tell them what had happened. But I didn't. How could I explain to them what I didn't understand or couldn't articulate? Though it couldn't of course be avoided for ever. Back in Edinburgh for a broadcast a few days later, Mum asked me how I'd found it, 'meeting your mother,' as she put it. She meant it well. She meant it as she expected me to feel it, but hearing those words coming from her I felt myself dying inside. I looked at her and I looked away. 'Oh, it was okay. Over and done with.' She looked at me and I looked away.

Pre-Dublin, I'd gone on so much about meeting my birth mother to my friends and colleagues that I had to find a way of deflecting the interest and excitement it generated among them. 'Oh it was mind-blowing. An incredible experience,' became my press release. 'It's strange but fascinating discovering all my Irishness.' Identity was one thing. The individual, quite another. It was an affirmation of my Celticness with an extra helping of romanticism, lyricism, rebel-hearted grievance – the grit in the oyster of 800 years of troubles.

But the Mother Stella was far more complicated than Mother Ireland. From the moment I flew home she was on to me and she wasn't going to relent. Clearly she thought this was the beginning and our relationship would grow as mother and son as it should have done had the vicissitudes of life not stopped it in its tracks. Now she wanted to make up for lost time. But my time hadn't been lost. I had my story – my truth. I'd met her, and it was unremarkable and underwhelming. As far as I was concerned, my quest was over. And while I understood her need and I didn't want to break off contact or never talk again – once every so often and a Christmas card would have been fine. Maybe even a trip to Dublin every couple of years – I wasn't up for what she was asking. I couldn't magic up feelings that weren't there. Maybe it was self-protection and subconsciously, I just couldn't let the hurt she'd already caused go deeper.

The most difficult thing in the world would have been to say, 'Please don't try and be what you are not. You are not my mum – my mummy. You are not even really my mother in any meaningful way. You are the someone who gave birth to me.' I didn't want to hurt her by saying that. Instead, the only way I knew how to deal with it was to say as little as possible. And anyway, I had to close it down for the sake of my sanity. My marriage was coming to an end, my mind was a mess and work was relentless and frenetic. I was hanging on in an ever-spinning wheel, by my fingertips.

My sanctuary, my haven of peace, was my *Into the Night* show on Radio 1. I was talking to the night from an eerily empty building, just beside Broadcasting House, in a smoke-swirling studio – because you could back then and I did back then, twenty a day – desk-lamp ambience, a pile of records and jingles by my side and my friend, the listener, a one-in-a-million out there somewhere. Every night was a new world of possibilities, depending on how I felt. I'd scrunch up and chuck away my producer's running order, run my fingers down the record shelf as I caressed the classics, flipped through the CDs and chose what magic we'd share. I played my mood, my state of mind, exposing my heart through the music – I felt an emotional connection with people through the songs I'd selected. Late-night radio promises an intimacy of exchange and in the same way I could sense the struggles of others, perhaps they could also hear mine. It wasn't me and them, it was us, together, two souls passing in the night, or that's what it felt like.

The feeling of saying something or playing something that made things just a little better for someone somewhere, or that related to their life in a magical way, could be unbearably moving and powerful. Playing 'Sunshine on

Leith' by the Proclaimers, a song so redolent of childhood in Edinburgh, one evening, I said: 'That's for you if you're on the late 33 bus from Leith heading for Edinburgh South right now,' the one I'd taken so many times, heading home. A week later I received a three-line letter from someone who had heard the song and been on the bus going home. She said it was a beautiful moment and she'd just stared out the window as the old stone houses and tenements rolled past.

Meanwhile, Stella's letters continued to arrive, the antithesis of the three-line simplicity of my listener. These pages were dense with words, the writing illegible, and it all required too much of an effort. What was the point of trying to decipher words that meant nothing anyway? I stopped bothering. They were about as cherished as pizza delivery leaflets, and about as welcome as unwanted bills. The letters would arrive and I'd bung them unopened and unloved in a drawer full of old biros, tickets and backstage passes. The letters didn't matter. They were anti-matter.

But they were the physical manifestation of how I felt – threatened by the link of them from me to her. If I read them, if I wrote back, I'd become more involved – drawn in and entrenched – a part of her world and she a part of mine in some one-to-one correspondence that would gradually un-adopt me. I'd gone as far as I could bear to.

The phone calls were another matter. I was used to talking, or hearing other people talk, and I could tune out mentally while letting her go on talking. They'd started a day or two after I got home, just to check I got back okay. The next and the next and the next were more problematic. 'IdidthisandthenIdidthatandwhathaveyoudonetoday and what plans have you got for the rest of the week and my friend came in earlier and we had tea and later I'm hoping to make some cheese on toast and that'll be nice hopefully anyway so tomorrow I am seeing Mary who lives near me . . .' Stella just wanted to talk. She didn't want to talk about anything – just to talk and have me talk back before she then talked again. Occasionally I tried pushing her into more interesting terrain, and she'd briefly talk about her family and parents, but never my birth father, who was a matter of some interest now that I knew her. She said she could 'barely remember' and always with an ever so slightly arch tone. I asked about her marriage and again the disaster of it was tersely expressed but never expanded upon. Back to cheese, on toast, off toast and much less complicated.

Whatever I'd unleashed I couldn't deal with it, and the calls started to unnerve me. I made excuses – bad timing, I was just about to go out; I was tired, sitting down after a long day of talking. Or it was past my bedtime. But she didn't give up. 'Hello. Nicky?' Timid but relentless. 'Err, hi. Stella. It's a bit difficult at the moment,' I'd say and suggest she call back 'next week or the week after.'

Having met her and now having her want a part of me, I found there was something about Stella's very essence that meant I could never imagine her being a mum. Never a parent. And anyway, this had never, for me, been about a mother upgrade. I'd been curious. I'd wanted to know, fill in a part of myself in the hope of filling a deeper, and the deepest, hole. I'd stopped needing her after she gave me the final bottle, and now that I'd met her, I'd stopped wanting so desperately to know and now I desperately wanted to move on. I didn't have the headspace for her – the life-space – the time for her. And, as my words from decades before came back to me, my lines of defence against tracing my birth mother: why would I want to find *her*? She gave me away, didn't want me, so why would I want to see her? – it hit me that the day she went to Ronnie Cameron, asking if he knew anyone who wanted to adopt a baby, was the beginning of the end. And the day she gave me my last feed and the social worker arrived to take me away to the baby home, however little choice she had, that was the day any obligation to her ended. She blew it. She had no claim on me. I wasn't the baby alone in the nursing home any more. I wasn't the confused little boy or the tortured teen-ager. I wasn't the reckless, agonised student. I was now in a position of strength. I wasn't bitter or angry. It was worse. I was indifferent.

But Stella was not one to give up, and before too long, amidst the blizzard of banalities, I became aware of one determined agenda. I'd heard it the first time I ever spoke to her; I heard it in the brief phone conversations before I closed them down and I'd seen it in the letters I'd read before we met. Deirdre. If you ever see Deirdre. I wonder if I'll ever hear from Deirdre, your sister. It was never 'my daughter'. Your sister. That was the lure, the moral imper-ative. It was down to me then? *Your sister?* More words to fry my brain. Wasn't having a parallel mother bad enough? I had no appetite for another genetic tornado sweeping through my life and anyway, wasn't it down to Deirdre?

Of course I was curious about her. Sharing genes and comparing notes on a trauma had its appeal; but then there might be two birth-people to emotionally cater for and I was pathetically failing with just the one. Tracing her might draw me into some Stella and ersatz daughter family circle, rather than my real family circle. If it happened, it happened. If Deirdre wanted to, Deirdre would do it.

Maybe strangely, given my reluctance to engage with Stella, extended family was a different kettle of connection though, and the one thing I did seem prepared to do was to meet Stella's nieces and nephew. These were my cousins and cousins were great. Cousins I could handle. Close enough to matter but not too close to challenge the mental status quo or further challenge the way I saw myself. There was an addictive fascination to finding out about and meeting extended family – a form of self-knowledge – and cousin Robert, a soon-to-be policeman in Dublin, was a huge support. He made me feel like a cousin, though it took him and his siblings a while to get the mind-blowing fact that 'Auntie Stella' had *children*. He didn't judge me on my lack of connection with his aunt, so I didn't need to lie about it. He tacitly understood the complexities and totally respected my right to know whatever I needed to and with no sense of 'who the hell are you?'

Robert filled me in with the occasional detail about Stella's life as well as his father's, Stella's adored brother Uncle John. He had looked out for and looked after his sister as much as he could all their lives, until he died suddenly, a bolt out of the black. Robert explained that his father had been Stella's protector, for that's what brothers are meant to be. She was devoted to him, her rock and support throughout her life when times were tough, and when John died she was broken. I don't know if he ever knew about her babies, but if she had told anyone it would have been John.

Her brother meant everything to Stella. In one of her first letters, she'd sent me a photo of him when he was a boy. I'd stared and stared. I thought it was me. It looked like one of the many photos of me as a little boy, squinting in the sun, looking slightly lost outside an old stone cottage. But it was an old black and white photo of my Uncle John on the farm where he grew up. That moment had been a different kind of belonging, because he was the first relative I'd ever seen who looked like me.

Robert had told me more about his dad being an Irish champion cyclist and a big wheel in the cycling establishment. Back in London, and having checked out my thigh muscles, I found myself inspired to spend a ludicrous amount of money on a racing bike I didn't have time to ride. I'd never had a bike. When I was a child Mum and Dad had been afraid I'd get killed on the main road, and the rare times I'd ventured into the growling London traffic on a borrowed bike as an adult, Lord of the Lycra, I had seen their point.

Talking to Robert I learned more about Stella, her lifelong battle with manic depression, the 'Spike Milligan one'. Either soaring through the clouds or plummeting into the wretched pits of despair. This all made sense to me – the wild abandon, impulsiveness, the choices she made, children she had. The lives she hid. There was something about this I instinctively understood – even recognised in some of my own behaviour and thoughts. I thought about it and then forgot about it.

I got phone calls whatever her mood, so when she called one day in a state of particularly high excitement, the words rushing out of her mouth like greyhounds, I held the receiver away like a stooge in an old comedy, the chipmunk ranting at arm's-length.

'Esther,' she said. '*Esther!*'

'Who's Esther?' My voice was flatter, ready with the I-don't-have-time-for-this.

'Deirdre. Deirdre. She found me. Somebody changed her name to Esther and Esther, *Esther* wants to speak to you. Nicky. *Esther.*'

She was blissfully breathless, unabated and un-inter-ruptible as she gabbled out what Esther had said, and what she had said, and then what Esther had said and what she had said.

In hearing her excitement, I realised that back in 1961 I was her second shot at having a child, but now in 1995, Esther was her second shot at having a child back. Esther had been over to see her. She had moved from Edinburgh and was now living near Bath. She was married with two children and she worked as a management consultant. They had spoken about me and Stella was now asking me if it was okay to give her my number. It was okay.

And so, when Esther rang a couple of days later, I didn't have to think how I should be. We just were. There was an ease as we spoke – and mutual amusement at how bizarre the whole situation was. I heard humour and intelligence, a reader-between-lines. I asked about her meeting with Stella and as I listened, I realised how similar our experiences had been. It wasn't just me, then. It wasn't totally my fault. Hearing this was a mighty relief and already I felt less alone.

We arranged for her to come to visit me a week or so later, at two p.m. The buzzer went at two p.m. This was good. She was punctual, an excellent start. I heard her footsteps coming through the lobby up the stairs, and there she was: my sister, a tall, angular, attractive woman with dark hair. Different colouring – different father. Same mother. Same city. Similar background. We embraced quickly like you're meant to otherwise you seem weird, and I could immediately see she was observing the scene, as well as being part of it. Me too. There were four of us there – two participants and two observers, both in the VIP seats. We all sat down.

'I thought you'd be taller,' she said, as if she'd been greeted by the Mayor of Munchkin City.

She too had her idealised fantasies – hers was a strapping six-foot-four-inch big little brother. As for my fantasy – I didn't expect her to look like she did, because she didn't look like me. I couldn't see me anywhere and I thought: I look more like Fiona. Was Esther sure she was Stella's daughter?

I was enjoying her company. She was wry and warm and we chatted about Edinburgh childhoods while looking at each other like we were in the Edinburgh zoo. Then, looking for clues, something struck me. I've got an unusually long second toe so I asked about her toes and our socks were off. It was a match. Right there was the Lackey foot. That meant more than anything – a tangible connection in a way that confounded all our knowledge and experience of the world. If those hominid feet were fossilised and excavated by anthropologists of the future, they would instantly know we were related.

I asked for her impression of Stella, and she literally did one. An impression of Stella's accent and demeanour, before describing their relationship thus far. Esther had encountered the same shallows and today was a massive relief for both of us. Like me she just expected someone different but like me she wasn't quite sure who. Like me, she'd weighed up all the ingredients: a successful professional woman – matron of a hospital – educated, independent, incredibly sexually liberated for late fifties Catholic Ireland. Mix all that up together and surely someone extraordinary came out of it all.

As with me, one of the first things Stella had asked Esther was if she liked animals. 'Do you like *animals*? Do you like *dogs*?' Irrespective of if she did or didn't – she did – Esther had found this to be a strange way to initiate a conversation with the child you'd given away thirty years previously. Unlike me, Esther hadn't lingered on the enquiry. It passed like a pylon on a train journey, because she had a battery of her own questions to ask and things to find out. A lifetime of mystery was there to be revealed. She needed time itself to stand still, then and now. She needed freeze-frame clarity, not riddles or platitudes.

I'd known Esther a matter of minutes before I sussed that she and Stella would never be a meeting of minds. Esther was one for diving into the deep-blue truth. We're not talking layers of neo-Freudian complexity here. It was basic stuff for someone who had a right to know. What was it like when you found out you were pregnant? Was there ever a possibility of keeping me? Who was my father? But if she wanted questions like that answered, she had the wrong mother.

Nothing but trifles. As with me, Stella was playing the part of being a mother with Esther in the most superficial yet cloying way. Esther was expecting more, but more never really came. Just as she thought it might, it didn't. It was just the same obfuscation – deflection and avoidance. The closed book with entire chapters redacted, erased and pulped, unwilling to reflect or explain.

More than anything, Esther was mystified. A mother's love is beyond words but even between the lines there was nothing. Meeting the sister formerly known as Deirdre was a huge relief in a big way. We had the same feeling of anticlimax after years of projecting and idealising. When I sheepishly – guiltily – explained how I was struggling with Stella's ongoing need to be part of my life and my inability to meet her needs and be some kind or any kind of a son, she got it. I felt less culpable. Less of a bastard.

But between us, we felt a bond. Siblings bond as they share lives and experiences growing up together, but ours was being swiftly forged from not growing up together, and from the similar expectations, experiences and feelings when we met our mutual mother. We were more than strangers with genes and second toes in common. All our lives we'd been looking into the same distance.

We swapped stories of growing up, our adopted families; of belonging, not belonging; who we were and who we weren't. And then we got on to schools and friends. She mentioned her best friend Julia, describing her house and their undying friendship, and making the connection I did a silent comedy double-take inside, suddenly realising she was talking about one of my best friends' big sisters. Matthew and Julia lived in an elegant stone detached house in one of the wide leafy roads of south Edinburgh. They had a kind of kids' lair-turned-teenagers' den off the kitchen with an L-shaped brown sofa against the wall and beanbags on the floor. It was the perfect speakeasy for smoky gatherings and preloadings, so my buddies and I were forever round there, loafing with swagger and self-regard.

I was excited by the link. I hope I didn't say 'what a small world', but I could well have. Esther was still talking. 'I even stayed with her for weeks one summer.' 'Which summer?' I asked.

'Oh it must have been around '78, '79.' She thought a moment. ''78. It was definitely '78.'

With that, I was right back in the den with Matthew and Iain, smoking Benson and Hedges, watching World Cup matches, lounging on the sofas, our feet on the beanbags. And through the smoky haze there was Julia; I could see her clearly, moving from room to room, coming in, fetching something and leaving. And her friend who was there – the one who always seemed to be there, brushing past the door like a ghost. I'd clocked her presence with fleeting curiosity and now, twenty-eight years later in a room in north London, here she was. My sister wasn't a face in the crowd on Princes Street, or on the bus or in the park. She'd been in other rooms in the same house, at the same time as me.

Esther laughed. She remembered Matthew's regular crew of too-cool-for-school scruffs – school ties halfway down their shirts, effing the afternoon away with their shoes kicked onto the floor. Just think if I'd had my socks off too.

When the mist clears and the faces emerge of the birth family, the people you've wondered about for as long as you've wondered, it begins to make sense and you get this sense of clarity. But with this clarity comes confusion. Are any of us who we used to be? Fiona knew about Stella – not that I ever discussed it with her – but no way could I tell Fiona about Esther. Her life and mine were so inter-twined by childhood – how could I even begin a conversation with the sister whose childhood I shared, if not her genes, about the one whose genes I shared, if not her childhood? So I bottled it and just mentioned Esther's sudden emergence to Mum, in an offhand way, so Fiona would get it second-hand. I knew she knew when she asked me: 'Are we who we used to be?' 'Yes!' I bellowed, as I writhed inside, her words like a harpoon to the heart. And changed the subject.

Adopted children learn to compartmentalise – that's me there and that's another me over there. Keeping everything separate makes you mad but keeps you sane. After meeting Stella and Esther, part of me now stood taller but another part was still curled up on the bed not knowing how to feel, battling against an eternal tussle to stay who I was, while embracing who I also was. I couldn't mix them and at times I needed to hide them, from myself and from others around me.

Six of the family: Isla, Tina, me, Breagha, Kirsty and Lilla, 2007

CHAPTER SEVEN

And I Love All of You

AT LEAST I'D *mentioned* Stella and Esther to Mum and Fiona. But when it came to Dad, I was unable to go anywhere near even uttering their names. I knew he knew I'd met them and I knew he would have respected and understood why this had been important to me, even something I had to do. But it would also have terrified him. He'd had a harsh upbringing, a tyrannical father carved from the cold stone of the nineteenth century, who'd stamped on his dreams of being an artist, and yet my dad had somehow emerged as a gentle, sensitive man, one to whom our family of four meant the world. And besides, I was so unequivocally 'his', there was nothing that needed discussing.

Since I was old enough to understand, he'd encouraged me to follow my dreams, to go in whichever direction I was heading. He was never going to be a father like his and he made it clear I could pursue my own life and make my own decisions and he'd always be there to support me. Tracing and meeting Stella had been a decision I'd made but somehow it was the one I couldn't share with him. When this decision and my dad came together in the same thought, I felt ashamed, disloyal, that I had, ultimately, failed him. More than that – after everything he and my mum had done for me it was as if I were discarding them and moving on. As if I was at last leaving the orphanage. Thank you. The staff were just marvellous and I'll never forget your kindness. Let's stay in touch. See you.

Even more of a justification for putting Stella away. Her letters lay unopened and her phone calls became less frequent. And when she did phone and I picked up, I now handed the phone to my new partner, Tina. She'd come into my life when she came into the studio to read the news. A no-nonsense journalist, full of immensely wonderful nonsense, fun, capable, compassionate, clever and loving, she was extremely tolerant of eccentricity and quickly came to understand the adopted child and his bothersome baggage. Difficult wasn't a deal-breaker and she loved all animals, especially dogs. If she hadn't it wouldn't have been my deal-breaker, but it saved me the effort of relentless evangelising before she saw the light. All was good. She took a good look at my picture of Candy, listened to the story of our love and had all sorts of theories about Toby's presence in Stella's room at the boarding house. 'Tina,' I told her, 'I just love dogs. That's all.' We vowed one day to have a house full of dogs and children but we'd go for the children first and the dogs would come along shortly after.

Soon after realising we were serious about each other, I took her to Edinburgh to meet my parents. Mum pulled out all the stops – cooking up a storm, serving it on the nicest plates, in the special room with the nice carpet, which was quite serious in itself. As we were clearing away the main-course cutlery, Dad passed me on the way back into the dining room and gave me his famous twinkling thumbs-up. He could tell how happy I was – the same son but a different person – and that made him happy. And Mum was a fan too. 'She's so *natural*,' she told me. 'What a lovely girl.' The fact they cared so much about who I was with and how happy I was reinforced my sense of belonging and, as I watched the three of them chatting as if they'd known each other for ever, I felt as secure as I ever had. After dinner, with the hushed reverential tones of a tour guide at the Holy Sepulchre, I took Tina to see Candy's chair in the upstairs front room. She completely got it and we both stood in silence for a moment looking out at the street, through Candy's eyes. And it just carried on getting better, so much so that by the time we left to go back to London, Tina felt like one of the family. And as they waved us goodbye, I was pretty sure that Mum, a lifelong atheist, was on the verge of screaming Alleluia, ready to run down the aisle banging a tambourine in the hope that we weren't far behind.

That weekend was special for very many reasons, not least because Tina was able to spend time with Dad. But the pains and digestive problems he'd been experiencing were becoming more intense. And when, a few weeks later, Mum phoned, calling to Dad to pick up the extension in the bedroom, I knew it wasn't going to be good news. 'It's pancreatic cancer,' said Mum, gently. 'It's terminal.'

Terminal. Such a curt and ugly word, and as Mum outlined what would happen next, the care he would receive 'meanwhile', in her calm, open and anguished way, I was struck by my dishonesty and the sheer treachery of my disavowal of all my dad had done for me; my self-absorbed flirtation with being someone I was never meant to be.

By the time I arrived in Edinburgh a few days later, Dad had taken a sudden turn for the worse and was in hospital. It was entirely possible, Mum told me, that the next move would be to the hospice for end-of-life care. The terminus. Walking into the ward in the Edinburgh Royal Infirmary, I saw him straight away, right across the shiny green floor in the last bed in the furthest corner. When I'd had my tonsils out, Mum and Dad had bought me a dinosaur book and as I saw him lying there, I was overwhelmed with wanting to give him something. But I'd come straight from the airport and was empty-handed. That felt bad. Maybe I could resurrect our joint love for Laurel and Hardy, the scene where Stan brings a hospitalised Ollie hard-boiled eggs and nuts, and say that was what I had brought with me for him. But when I got close and saw how weak he was, I couldn't find any words.

When I reached his bed, Dad opened his eyes. He looked different – vulnerable, smaller – and I realised it was because he wasn't wearing his glasses. His glasses were him – his glasses were so much a part of what he looked like, and it was one of those surreal moments when you see a face you know so well but it seems like the first time. He smiled. In the light of his eyes, I caught the sparkle of his love for me and as I took his hand, my love for him was never more focused and concentrated. When I spotted his spectacles crouching on his bedside table on top of the *Telegraph* crossword, I felt a huge surge of relief; in spite of everything, a stay of execution, and I was finally able to speak.

We chatted gently for a while, the usual reductive banalities of hospital chit-chat: logistics – the bed was too far from the door; the ambience – the ward was noisy at night; the care – the nurses were kind. I caught sight of the morphine drip, a catheter and wires feeding him saline solution.

'Fancy a pint, Dad?' He smiled, a perfect proxy for a belly laugh. I smiled back. So much better than hard-boiled eggs and nuts.

Inside I was in free-fall, the manic side of me clamouring wildly, amidst the sterile claustrophobia. I wanted to say something strange at the top of my voice. I wanted to boom, 'And death shall have no dominion' like Richard Burton. I wanted to sprint up and down the ward touching the wall at one end and desk at the other and spin around. But I held on to his hand as he drifted in and out of sleep, the morphine drip clicking. This was my chance. 'Dad. You know when I traced my birth mother, it was only because I needed to know once and for all who she was so I would never need to know again. I thought about you and Mum all the time while I was meeting her, and no part of her, no part of me meeting her, was relevant to our real lives. And through it all – tracing her, meeting her, talking to her – I felt ungrateful, mortified. I felt like a traitor, a double agent and I didn't speak to you about it because I wanted to protect you. Like you protected me from the day you went to Ronnie Cameron and found out about me, to right this moment, now.' But I was a coward. And as I thought it, I couldn't say it, as he lay there at the last stop before the terminal.

He opened his eyes, temporarily, momentarily, clear from pain. With as much strength as he could muster, he pointed to the shelf behind him and the card I'd sent home a few days before.

'I love that, Nicko. That's what I love.'

He put his thumbs up, beaming in silence. His naked eyes were glistening. All I'd written was 'I love you'. I'd said it before and written it before, but now it seemed to mean more to him than anything I'd ever said to him in my life. Maybe it was okay and all the things I wanted to say, and should have said, were wrapped up in those three words. But later, when I kissed him goodbye – for now – still those long-lurking regrets were raging inside and I felt ashamed.

Then I was shaken back to the moment – halfway back down the row of beds a voice called out to me. 'Hey pal,' said an old man. 'Come over here, pal.' I glanced over. He was frail, like a skeleton with sunken pleading eyes, in the last gasps of life, an oxygen mask hanging limp beside the bed. His voice, strong and insistent, was still raging against the dying of the light. Back at the far end Dad's eyes were closed and a nurse was taking his blood pressure. He was the kindest person I think I ever knew, with a massive heart and endless time for anyone and everyone. Both of my parents had a burning interest in people from every walk of life. Dad couldn't stand people who turned their noses up at others or were dismissive. Whatever the circumstances he'd stop to talk. And this man lay alone, and the alone-ness of him was more acute than any fight for breath. Apart from the twelve weeks I was alone after my adoption, when Mum and Dad were waiting for me, I'd had someone there for me all my life, and now with Tina and me possibly having family one day, someone would be there for me right up until the moment I drifted off, tubes snaking everywhere, in some hospital bed. I sat down in the bedside chair. I tweaked my accent twenty per cent.

'How you doin?'

'Fighting fit son,' he gasped. 'Fighting fit.' He was only half joking. Somewhere inside he was fighting fit. Standing on the terraces at Easter Road, puffing away on his Navy Cut Full Strength, pound-for-a-packet-of-twenty-the-world's-gone-fucking-mad, watching the Hibs with a meat pie and a Bovril at half-time and a few pints on the way home. Fighting fit. I asked him if he needed anything and in a whispery rasp he indicated that he was okay.

I told him I was here seeing my father and I'd be back tomorrow and we had a couple more moments of hospital chit-chat. 'I'll see you tomorrow,' I said, like it was already in the diary.

'Yes, see you tomorrow.'

I had done my best, but Dad would have done it so much better.

Death was close. Within days Dad was being moved to the hospice. He asked to spend a couple of hours at home on the way there from the hospital. They'd had the upstairs bathroom decorated and he wanted to sit there for a while and admire the finish and then he wanted to sit in every room in the house, the rooms reverberating with memories and love. There had been a lot of both, forty-three years' worth of it, to be precise. In the hospice I held on to his hand and told him we all loved him. Then, and it sounded like a final goodbye, a full stop, he said: And I love all of you.

I promised myself that whatever my failings, and there were many, if I could at least strive to be half the man he was, I would achieve a lot. Family was at the epicentre of everything for him. He'd made us safe and we'd made him complete; he'd rescued me and we'd protected him from the phantoms of his past, the ghouls of war. Just thinking about him made me a calmer, better person and when the time came for me to have my own children, I knew I had the greatest role model to emulate.

And I knew too that I wanted to have that family with Tina, and so, soon after Dad's death, on a trip to the Highlands, after an intrepid walk down a mountain path to the sea, as we sat on the sand listening to the seabirds and the roaring waterfall at the bottom of the hill, I popped the big question. 'Yes,' she said. And then, 'Do you have a ring?' I didn't but I thought fast. 'It's here,' I said. 'We're sitting in it. It's the diamond sparkling stream winding its way round to the sea. The Ring of Bright Water.' We sat in the late-afternoon sun, in the most beautiful place in the world to me, watching the waves. It was the place where Gavin Maxwell had written the books I'd fallen in love with and where he had dreamt of one day finding his perfect idyll safe from the hectic angst and neurotic complexities of the world outside, and on that late-autumnal day, from late morning until the golden hour, everything was perfect, not another human being in sight.

By then we were already living together, the smooth but rapid segue from a night here and a night there. Still feeling so raw after losing my dad, I found the prospect of engaging with Stella and letting her into my life in one of her less frequent, but still endless, calls even more uncomfortable. I hadn't said what I wanted or needed to say to Dad and still felt that it was tantamount to cold-shouldering Mum, who was, heartbroken but stoic, in the process of getting life back on track. She would never have seen it that way but I did. Tina understood all that without a word being spoken and it befell her to stand at the gate, a benign sentry. She and Stella sometimes spoke for up to an hour about nothing but everything. I was in a strange netherworld, feeling that Stella was being looked after and made welcome, but I was being kept remote and safe.

Anyone who has experienced it says that the moment you become a parent you know it's the most powerful, existentially, mind-bogglingly magical experience. It's a coming of age and self-revelation. Every adopted person I've spoken to who has become a parent to their biological child says that non-adopted people will never understand what it feels like. We are on the peaks of two different mountains and while the views are both breathtaking, they are slightly different. Holding our daughter Breagha in my arms for the first time was an astonishing and profound moment that took me to many lifetimes and so many different roads. Her lifetime and mine, to Stella's, to Mum's, to Dad's, to the people whose decisions, mistakes, luck and love led me to this point. She was a part of me, she belonged to us and no one was going to come and take her away.

I had a child. I actually had a child. Part of me. Not a stranger in a hotel foyer but someone I helped create from nothing, with someone I loved. I wanted to be everything to her – all the things Dad was to me. He let me go my own way, make my own mistakes, was worried about me, proud of me, ambitious for me – not in a materialistic way but in wanting me to be as happy in life as I could possibly be, knowing he and Mum would always be there for me, I wanted to lift her up and blow a giant raspberry on her neck, just like Dad had done with me, and hear her fountains of laughter.

Having my own child set off all sorts of triggers in me, making me think of what had come before and before that and before that. And it struck me that there was still a missing link and that I needed to fill it because that heritage was her right to know. At some point I'd be the future version of Dylan Thomas's 'yellowing dicky-bird watching pictures of the dead'. They will know me or know of me. She had that same right. That, for her, would never threaten to compromise who she was as it had for me. It would mean a picture of the past but not one that would in any way colour her present.

Imagine going your entire life knowing you had a child out there somewhere. I imagined it. Stella told me that my birth father knew I'd been born. Partly for Breagha's legacy and partly for my curiosity, I decided that I would find out who he was and what he felt about it all. I could never have embarked on the search while Dad was alive, and even now it felt right to do it and wrong to do it. Ultimately I didn't feel I was insulting his memory because unlike last time, I was completely clear in my own mind why I was doing all this. Compared to the last time I was coming from a position of strength, and there had never been any attachment issue going on – no sense of abandonment, conscious or otherwise.

There is something about tracing a birth mother that seems a natural obvious genetic gravitation, necessary and understandable because of what a mother is – the source and sustainer of life. Tracing her is understandable, but tracing him raised all sorts of questions, not least why bother? Precisely because my dad was my dad, and after everything I'd learned from the last time, I had the confidence to proceed and be invulnerable. My birth father had never provoked my curiosity in the same way, not even had a walk-on part in the myth of my creation. I'd never really thought about him. There would be and could be none of the confusions or baggage of last time. He was the father, not my father, and if it turned out well that was a bonus; but a little bit of knowledge would go an awful long way for me.

I didn't know his name. If I could get it from Stella that would give me a fighting chance. Perhaps selfishly, that was a call I did make. She had no idea what had become of him but she gave me the name. 'If you ever do manage to find him,' she said, a serrated tone to her voice, 'he has a book of poetry of mine and I'd kindly like it back.'

Again, a private detective unpicked the lock of the mystery and in I went and this is what I discovered, on paper and then more later, when I went to meet him: he lived in the depths of rural Ireland, was in rude health – well over a cancer scare – and still relatively young, in his early sixties. When I was born, Stella had been thirty-six and he just twenty-three, which added still more colours to the picture. He was a roguish wit, a politically committed Irish patriot – 'I don't watch British TV,' he told me several times – and was entertainingly larger than life. He was nothing like Dad, but then he wasn't my dad. His children were great, considering how I bashed the door down like the cops on a dawn swoop; one phone call changed a lot of stuff and for me, not to be rejected was to be warmly embraced. My imprudent conception long pre-dated his marriage, so all was well there – or as far as it could be.

He'd known about Stella's trip to Edinburgh and why she had to go but, a master of discretion and looking after number one, he had never mentioned it to another soul, so his subsequent offspring had a bit to take in and take on; but they did.

'I sometimes thought about you right enough,' he told me. 'Wondered how you were getting on.'

I respected and liked that because it was honest, and that meant a lot. There was no tortured expression of lifelong angst or feelings of guilt; no 'oh my son at last you've found me' and hammy tears of redemption. But crucially, there was no denial. He was 'delighted'. I hadn't been an aching sorrow but at least I was an unexpected, happy development.

His deep self-defining Irishness was all those history and politics books embodied and personified – the ones I'd bought when I met Stella, which I'd gone on to read, voraciously. But he was so much more than a pile of Irish history books beside my bed. He was a chronicler, a database. With his knowledge and fire it was like he'd leapt off the page. He was interesting, and he was interested, as I was too, and thought it right, indeed vital to tell me about my 'culture'. He believed all that hand-me-down hurt was a birthright and a gift and the heritage of grievance was his gift to me. Part of my bloodline, birthright and nationhood.

By the time we met, Tina and I had had two more daughters, Lilla and Kirsty – the fourth hadn't as yet appeared on the scene – and he said of Lilla, with all the Celtic romanticism he could muster: 'The shape of her face, the look in her eyes – I tell ya – she could only be from the West Coast of Ireland.' I was cool with that, another mark of my not mutually exclusive senses of identity. His emotional connection with my family was all about the bigger picture.

And Stella. Stella too delighted in the birth of my children, sending them birthday and Christmas presents – often things she'd knitted – and Tina sent a photo of the kids every Christmas – smiling little faces that could only have come from Clapham, or Tina actually, as luck would have it for them. When they were very little, we went to Bath to see Esther and her family. She'd got Stella over to stay and with so much more to know and discover, for a fleeting moment I thought that having her in this different setting would be perhaps a better way to explore each other's lives. But the day was a blur of miscommunication and lots of little children fractious at having to be watched in an unfamiliar setting, and later Esther told me she'd found the weekend oppressive and her sense of dislocation from Stella a sobering depressing reality. It was a somewhat reassuring reality for me though in that I felt the sins of the wayward son somewhat expiated.

And when we explained to the girls about Stella – Daddy came out of another mummy's tummy but Granny is his mummy – they, with the innocence and unintended candour of small children, found it irrelevant and uninteresting. Why would they not? They'd never been abandoned. They weren't imposters. And as far as they were concerned, Mum was their real granny, the granny who they adored, and she gave them all the love in the world and I saw it all and felt it all again, like I was the little child she was loving. And with the birth of Isla, our fourth and final daughter, in 2004, the fortification of family made me feel safer than I ever had.

So I could finally make sense, even if there were a lot of us, of my extended family. There was a birth father and his family; my birth mother and her birth daughter – my birth sister, my Bath sister; there was my actual mum and sister and the abiding memory of Dad. And then there was Tina and our daughters – my own family. The imposter is always lurking but I got on with my own family life, providing and nurturing. The other stuff – the searching and discovering – that was it. That was done. I knew what I knew. The disquiet was temporarily quietened.

Echoing down Whitehall, 2011

CHAPTER EIGHT

The Perfect Mother

QUIETENED BUT NOT silent and never quite still. And, maybe cocooned by having my own family now, I began to speak publicly about being adopted, tracing my birth mother and father. And once I started – on my radio phone-in, interviews on TV, in newspapers and magazines – I couldn't stop. Not so much talking but listening, as so many people began to share their experiences with me. It was as if I had joined a conversation that had been ongoing for years and I was startled by hearing the stories like mine, by so many similar feelings, in what felt like an extended family of waifs and strays; a virtual orphanage filled with adopted children like me. 'That's just how I felt,' said voice after voice, a comforting overture to a thousand exchanges, everyone's story the same, but all of them so different.

Once I was 'out' I was invited to work with the British Association of Adoption and Fostering and other campaigning groups, and Esther and I even gave a couple of talks together to share and hear experiences of being adopted, our similar upbringings, being strangers in the same city and then tracing Stella and finding each other. And we helped each other articulate our similar feelings about the challenges of reality – a real birth mother, a real person and unreal expectations. And I became immersed in it, this adoption roadshow, talking to adopted people and adoptive parents, sometimes in a room, often from a stage or a studio, into a microphone or TV camera. I loved it and it felt so good.

But there was a growing gnawing paradox. The more I spoke, the more exposed I felt and the more exposed I felt, the more the old feelings returned, that sense of alienation and isolation, the meaning of family and all the complex lifelong contradictions of adoption, of being an imposter in my own life, of having been rejected and abandoned. My swords of truth were double-edged. I was truly me, out and proud and loud, but I was truly exposed; naked in the spotlight, and I began to imagine that people were pointing at me, seeing me for what I was, or wasn't – he's not real; he's an imposter – and my own child within was running wild. The shame of adoption always there, always a part of me, reared up and would not be quietened.

Mum came to a talk I gave in Glasgow. As I finished telling the story of my and Esther's uncannily similar second toes, I spotted her laughing along with everyone else at the image of two long-lost siblings examining each other's gnarled feet. It was a powerful moment, a fleeting vignette of total unconditional love. I told the audience that she was there and she received a spontaneous round of applause, which delighted her. She waved hello back to everyone and at the meet and greet afterwards people queued up to meet her, which she loved. On the way home she laughed again as she mentioned that somebody had told her I certainly had 'a touch of the Blarney-Stone'.

It was a cathartic process. The more public I was about my adoption, the more I talked about my parents and how I 'won the lottery' on the day Mum and Dad adopted me. Being able to explain out loud why I needed to trace Stella, and having the chance to celebrate my family and wonderful childhood, in the full shining glare of the sun was something I should have said yes to and done for my parents years before. It lifted a massive cloud of guilt.

I was candid about the contrast between the birth mother I'd imagined and the one I'd met, but I tried to explain as sensitively as I could the context of the times and the challenges she faced in a world with too much religion and too little sympathy and compassion. The mere fact that she gave away two babies in the space of eighteen months hit me every time I said it. The fact that it was the best thing that ever happened to me was implicit. I didn't embellish and I didn't lie.

The people I spoke to were understanding, non-judgemental. Many had gone through similar experiences. But outside that acceptance, it wasn't so straightforward. There were consequences to being public. I was open, obviously, about the fact that Stella was from Dublin, and journalists – like private detectives – don't hang around when they need to track someone down. One Irish tabloid published a horrible article, portraying her life with a morally judgemental conservatism. Fortunately she was shielded from it, inside the care home she was living in, by now suffering with Parkinson's disease and occasionally confused – that is, until another journalist from one of the 'usual suspect' franchises blagged her way in, flourishing flowers, pretending to be a relative. When the care home manager told me the journalist had popped in as a 'family member', I wondered if I was actually just as phoney as that tabloid hack. I felt terrible that I'd unleashed those hounds, but I also knew Stella had been protected when the care staff had given the hack her marching orders, and as such she hadn't really clocked what was going on.

As her health declined, Esther and I went over together to visit a couple of times and she was so happy to see us. In the care home she was a sweet and gentle version of herself, with a palpable inner contentment and maybe even a sense of personal redemption because we were actually both there in the room with her. Maybe for her everything had worked out in the end. But she was still inscrutable, the feisty bossy hospital matron, when it came to talking about the past. For Esther it was mission impossible getting any information about her own birth father, however tactfully she broached it; her line of questioning was hardly an interrogation, but it was always brushed away.

And then, on 14 September 2008, Robert called me to say she had died. We were there at the beginning and we were there at the end. Esther and I went over for her funeral on a bleak Dublin day. We both did readings and as I helped carry her coffin, I thought about the body it contained and how it had once contained me, a macabre Russian doll of death.

Esther and I were both conscious that there was no explanation at the funeral as to who we were. Although everybody knew, nobody said, and everyone, apart from Robert and his family, who were welcoming and embracing, regarded us like we were illegitimate children, which of course we were. There I was, the bastard son; there Esther was, the unwanted daughter. And if no one else was thinking it, I was sad – but not sad enough.

I thought they thought it was shocking we'd had the temerity to reappear, and I caught more than a trace on the cold autumn wind of the stifling judgement that had led to two babies being born in Edinburgh to a pregnant nurse in the first place. And the second place. Ghosts of a bygone time but ghosts of real flesh and blood.

The wake was full of people who looked like me and that made the rejection I felt even more painful. A stranger to my own tribe. There was an uncle there, the living brother of Stella. As he talked energetically to the gaggle of people around him, one of whom was me, I said something friendly but he just carried on talking. I wasn't even a passing curiosity. The adopted child wanted him to be warm and welcoming but he didn't even look in the pram. Why should he? I wasn't meant to happen and now he knew about me he could see that a lot of his sister's problems were all my fault. I was a paranoid pariah, and my birth mother's funeral was an adoption anxiety nightmare from start to finish.

A week or so later I was at Fiona's place in Perthshire. 'I'm sorry about what happened,' said my brother-in-law Ray. 'We were thinking about you.' I didn't know what he was referring to, so much had I already locked it all away. He looked confusedly at my confusion. 'Stella,' he said, gently. He used her first name, which made me feel uncomfortable. I didn't know he even knew it. And I realised that I thought he mistakenly thought that this death was as big for me as my dad's or my grandpa or Candy's. But it wasn't. Things were more complicated than that. Stella's death was a different kind of death, far too complicated to ever understand.

'Ah yes. Well. You know,' I wittered back 'That's. The way . . . it is.' And I put it back, away in a box. Safe from harm. Like the letters. Like the leaflets. I was born. She moved on. She died. I moved on because survival depended on it.

While I wasn't overcome by the sort of overwhelming sadness that invaded every part of me when my dad died, I was rather more disturbed by Stella's death than I at first realised. She had died, but nothing else about what she did back in that Edinburgh boarding house had changed. She had still abandoned me. I was still an adopted child, still searching for answers. In all the time I had known her, I had never heard anything like an adequate answer as to why she had left me. Nor had she shown any interest in the life my parents had given me. And now my questions would never be answered and she could never ask me the questions I needed to answer either. The aftermath of her death was not grief and yet I felt brittle and fragile, teetering on the edge of something, without quite understanding why.

And so it was that one summer's evening, the light bright through the curtains, the family downstairs still enjoying the late sunshine, I was in bed and unable to sleep, my

3.45 a.m. alarm set for the morning radio news programme I'd been co-presenting on BBC 5 Live for the past few years. The panic persistent, I put on the TV and with the express desire to only sleep, I started to watch a documentary that followed the lives of a particular herd of the Amboseli elephant herds in Kenya. The star of the show was Echo, the matriarch, and within seconds, I was mesmerised by this vision of maternal perfection.

I knew elephants were smart, but the sheer range and depth of cognition and emotion in Echo was the most heart-stoppingly beautiful thing I'd ever seen. Echo the matriarch, in her humbling magnificence, was the heart of her family's world – selfless, wise, patient, possessing this deeply formed and driven sense of duty. She led and protected because she knew no other way. At the birth of a baby, a grandchild, there came a trumpeting of collective joy from the whole family, filling the savannah, a celebration of welcome and belonging. They understood birth all right.

At every turn Echo's first concern was family. One of her daughters had been speared and I watched as Echo and other members of the herd leaned against her physically, helping her stay on her feet. They belonged so perfectly and unconditionally to each other and as the programme finished, I fell into a troubled sleep, and when the early morning came I'd dreamt I'd been awake all night. I was too clumsy to explain to myself what I was feeling. It lay somewhere else.

I kept going. I had responsibilities and, while the early start every day exacerbated any vulnerabilities, the exhilarating mania of live radio masked them, albeit temporarily.

That three-hour buzz gave me wings every day but the crash-landing could be brutal. One morning as I came off the air, I noticed we'd received several messages commenting on a 'right verbal pummelling' I had received. Oblivious to what this referred to, I asked a colleague, who told me that the evening before, while I was fast asleep, a certain comedian had randomly laid into me on his TV show, with a stream of vicious obscenities, some graphic. I hauled myself home and watched. He'd laced his words – pungent phrases – together for comic effect like a kind of performance poem and every toxic syllable, Dylan with malice, jabbed into me and dragged me into the dark. I watched it again and again. I couldn't not watch it. And every time I saw how the audience laughed I crumbled a little bit more – and then I played it again. This was it. Now they all knew that I was an imposter. I didn't belong, nor did I deserve to. They could all see I was worthless. They were right and he was right. I went to bed, pulled the covers over my head and I stayed there, dead to myself.

Thoughts repeated themselves on a perpetual loop like a punishment from some Greek myth; molehills became mountainous and I could never quite push the boulder to the top. Instead of looking inwards to the source of my distress, I mounted the barricades to fight external irritations. The first of these was the scourge of litter.

Litter had always irritated and confused me, but now I become obsessed. Things carelessly, wilfully discarded, blighting the world for others. People uncaring, not even caring that they were, and not able to see the best of the world, the beauty of nature even though it was staring them in the face. I took to chasing – and confronting – people who dropped litter in plain sight. If I couldn't chase them I would photograph them in the act; all the better if there was evidence and clues as to who they were and where they worked. I moved around as if I were compiling a file for Britain's Most Wanted.

Coming back from town one afternoon, I came out of the tube a stop early so I could walk across the park, my litter antennae twitching. When I spotted a massive pile of empty bottles and pizza boxes, dumped like a bespoke landfill, across the way, I broke into a run, leaping toward them. And yes, oh yes, as I got nearer, I could see they'd made a fatal mistake – receipts from a local off-licence. I had them. I bloody had them. There was bound to be CCTV and the shop would have a credit card record of who they were. I gathered the evidence, stuffing the damning confetti of receipts into my pocket, and strode back home.

In the living room, I laid the receipts out across the table and sat down for a closer look. Let the forensics begin, I thought as I opened a page in my notebook, practically licking the tip of my pen. I'll nail each and every one of these sinners. I set to work. Columns, rows, timings. I hadn't noticed Tina come in. She asked me what I was doing and I explained as if it was the most normal thing in the world. 'And so, when I've detailed all these, I'll go over to the off-licence before I get the police involved.'

This wasn't the first time. She sat down, looked through some of the receipts with me and then calmly talked me down, diverting my attention and refocusing me on to the things that really mattered, bringing me back to the children and love. It worked, for the time being anyway, and I re-gathered the receipts and put them in the recycling bin outside. A better outcome, at least, than them being left on the grass.

One of us needed to do something about this and Tina had obviously been reflecting more on how to help me because a couple of weeks later, there she was in the hall with her fleece on, about to go out 'to see my friend Sarah.' I wasn't really focusing but when I heard the word litter, I perked up.

'Litter?'

'A litter of puppies. And I've already got my eye on one.'

Calm, clear and casual. She was a newsreader and she should have announced this as if it was at the top of the news bulletin – breaking news, or what used to be called a newsflash – but she said it as if she were asking me to pass the Hellmann's, or saying that she was off to the shops. She knew there had to be no time for objection, that this was a unilateral and final decision, that this was now, finally, time for the dog we had always promised ourselves but never quite been able to fit in around four young children and our busy work lives; and in this she was right. She knew what Candy meant to me, our life and his death, that this dog in the photo on my desk was central to my sense of who I was and that now, in the place where my mind had found itself, I needed that unfathomable special extra dimension in my life more than ever.

'That's mad,' I said and before she asked if taking discarded till receipts to the police wasn't, I asked, 'What kind of dog?'

'A Labrador,' she said. She had her coat on and was dangling the car keys like a jailer doing the rounds. She was going to set me free – or keep me somewhere safe. She smiled and walked out the front door.

Maxwell comes home, 2008

CHAPTER NINE

Brown-Eyed Boy

ALL THE GOOD, bad and sad things were spin-cycling through my mind. But mostly a kind of exhilarated bewilderment. I just couldn't believe that, on this day that had come from nowhere, thirty-five years after I'd lost my best friend I was going to get another dog.

The children were old enough and the sofas were too, but this was such a step into the unknown that I was frightened by the reality of it. Candy and I had been as one and I knew I couldn't just acquire a ready-made factory-setting soulmate. If this new dog and I were going to be brothers, I'd need to be a child again. On reflection that was doable; but would he mean the same to me as Candy had? Would he love me like Candy did? He might gravitate towards the children and I wouldn't get a look-in. And then, the graver problem: how would I make him safe and make sure he remained alive? I even wondered if I was being disloyal to Candy in some way by opening my heart to another dog.

I was a mangle tangle of anxiety like a father-to-be in one of those black and white films, pacing anxiously back and forth, waiting for news of delivery of a new member of the family.

Throughout that long day, I kept seeing the picture on my desk – the black and white shot of Candy, alert, ears pricked up and looking straight down the lens. Whoever took that photo had called his name and timed it beautifully, in a second-from-the-sixties, preserved for ever. And that image I'd carried around in my mind for as long as I could remember was everywhere I looked. 'Boy on carpet with dog' – an adopted child and his best friend, *Playschool*, *Blue Peter* and *Doctor Who* flickering in the corner, and the two of us on a faded green carpet in our impregnable invincible secret world.

And as the day wore on and on and on, I became more and more convinced that not only would this dog be able to love me, but that I would be able to love him. And what a life we would give him. Our dog would also have a special chair and his dog hairs would be everywhere. Our dog would have great walks in the Scottish hills. Our dog would be the best cared for, most loved dog. Our dog would be my dog. And I would be his. We'd be there for each other.

Three long hours later, Tina called. Her hands-free motorway voice was several octaves higher than when she'd left and there was a Labrador on board. It was in the cage that had been surreptitiously purchased, hidden in a groaning shed I never looked in and placed by dead of night in the back of the car I never drove.

'Wait till you see him,' squeaked Tina. 'It was meant to be.'

It was meant to be? Just like me. He was a he who was meant to be and she was bringing him home, and maybe even me as well. But then I panicked. She'd taken him from his mother and the only world he'd ever known and he was on his way to south London.

'How is he?' I could barely hear my own voice.

'He's fine,' she said. 'I'm bringing him home.'

Later, she told me he'd cried all the way home. But the parting had only been hard for him, an eight-week-old puppy. His mother, Cara? Her time with her son was over. She'd sat on the gravel drive looking at the car as it drove away, but there had been no anxious maternal reflex when her puppy was taken, as there would have been in previous weeks. For Cara now, those feelings were fading to black, almost gone, evolved for survival. She just carried on. When Tina's car was out of sight, she'd wandered indoors and continued with her enviously untroubled and uncomplicated life.

And so, enter Maxwell. He arrived at 3.30 p.m. on 4 July 2008 and then it was real again. The gate clanged open, the key slotted into the lock and the door opened. Tina stood there beaming with this adorable blond ball of puppy in her arms. He was crying and looking round wildly, wondering what the hell this was all about now. But every part of Tina was jubilant. She held him out. 'What do you think?' she asked, assuming that's what I was doing. But I wasn't doing any such humdrum mental processing. I was somewhere else – way beyond. I was being, living, feeling.

Maxwell's distress was an echo of my own life, another emotional reflex that ensured the protective part of me kicked straight in and wanted to make everything okay for him. As soon as Tina placed him on the floor, I knew exactly what to do. I lay on the rug at his eye level to reassure him, and he suddenly gained some confidence and rushed towards me like a tiny bull in a world of china. As soon as I got his puppy smell it was overpowering – wafting over me like crop spray from the Elysian Fields. I felt tipsy. A giddying rush of something wonderful and new. That elixir of childhood.

I put my head near his and, without thinking, snuffled at him as dogs do when they're happy to see you. Our instant connection was extraordinary; something suddenly made perfect sense to both of us. His language was my first language from before I could even walk, let alone talk; from before anyone was able to explain to me that I wasn't actually a dog and Candy wasn't my real brother.

And then the children arrived home from school and despite the need for calm, there was a Campbell carnival – a pulsating fiesta of happiness, with a ticker tape parade thrown in when he broke loose and got his paws and jaws on the newspaper's Culture section. He was loving the attention, excited but obviously still so confused about this strange new world. By teatime, he was indeed Maxwell – named after Gavin Maxwell, the author of my treasured *Ring of Bright Water* and also for my favourite Beatles song, 'Maxwell's Silver Hammer'. But honestly, mainly because Maxwell just was his name. When my two youngest girls asked me why I'd called him Maxwell and I told them that was the name his mother Cara had given him, they both looked relieved.

He slept for much of the rest of the afternoon. I was early to bed, as ever, and as I went off to sleep there was no uncertainty, no catastrophising, no fear. This had been a red letter, blue riband, yellow Labrador retriever puppy day. A wonderful day. But when Tina came up to bed and that lonely agonising whimpering downstairs began, I was tortured. He needed me. I needed him.

'He's a dog, not a baby,' said Tina.

'But he's a baby that's just been taken away from his mother,' I said, bitterly. '*You* don't know what that's like.' There was no reply to this emotional howitzer and who-knows-how, she soon fell asleep, breathing gently. The sweet sighs of Morpheus. Bloody lucky her. To hell with all that 'he's just a dog' stuff though – I wanted to rush downstairs. But as much as it was killing me, I knew she was right and I made myself stare at the ceiling, knowing that if I did, he'd cotton on to it and use crying as a cue for us to go downstairs – like a butler's bell.

Within ten seconds of the 3.45 a.m. alarm, about twelve hours since he'd arrived, I was heading downstairs with not a thought of getting ready for work. I walked into the dark kitchen. He was still whining a poignant little whine, but then he registered my presence and for a second was still as a statue. Who did he want me to be? Where did he want to be? Once I'd turned the light on and he saw who I was, he came clattering across the cage towards me. I opened the door and picked him up and he recognised my smell and was calm. We were already in the land of magic. I was the one who loved him already and we both knew that everything was going to be okay.

From that morning, he turned to me whenever he saw me, he looked for me when he couldn't see me and he became the most wonderful companion. From those first hours he took me back to a feeling of security, reassurance and innocent joy. The time we share with dogs, that bond we have, is heartbreakingly brief, precious and fragile, but your heart never forgets. Maxwell had arrived and for the second time in my life, I was safe. I knew in a heartbeat of our connection that those gnawing feelings of abandonment that have never really left me, furtively whispering or even taunting me throughout my life, were not going to floor me. They were not going to bring everything down on top of me because I could be with Maxwell like I had been with Candy.

As Maxwell grew and was trained – although that description is stretching it – our bond grew ever stronger. Tina and all our girls were crazy about him, making up little poems and songs and creating colourful portraits of our newest family member with differing standards of brushwork. But from that first day and night, it was me he attached himself to at that fiercest, deepest level, and from then on, when things were bad I longed for him. That mutual attachment between Maxwell and me – dogs and us – remains one of the treasures and wonders of life.

I looked around and he was sitting by my feet. I'd go upstairs and he'd follow me; on the sofa he'd be up there with me, leaning his head against mine. Down on the floor and he wanted to play, so we played. And over time, as he invited me to share in his world, we got to know each other and he brought back to me – and brought out in me – that empathy and mutual reliance I'd had with Candy. In the thirty-five intervening years I'd loved and sought out dogs at every turn, but the feeling of having Maxwell, *my* dog, was unsurpassable. As our lives grew together and we walked across the London commons and up Scottish mountains as my mind cleared after my morning show or a trip to the other side of the world, or we sat together in my study as I worked, an inner calm began to settle on me.

Only those with a strong mutual bond with an animal can properly understand what it means and how it feels. Dogs bring out the best in us because they make us reach beyond the confines of humanity into an enchanted realm. On the occasions when I've presented phone-ins or discussions about dogs, people are so relaxed. In their voices I can hear a sense of wonder it is impossible to properly articulate, the feeling of liberation from being merely human. There is so much more to this wonderful life.

And the dog lovers, knowingly or otherwise, have stumbled upon a priceless truth – human beings don't actually monopolise the capacity to love and those who can move beyond that have been given a golden ticket to another world. Dogs work their wonders on a deep emotional level and we know instinctively why they do and how they do, but when we demand logic, words invariably fail and it's the heart that prevails. That's all that matters.

Maxwell is a very special boy and within a matter of moments, there had never been a dog so cherished and such a part of the family as him, a walking wagging reservoir of infinite love, busy enriching all our lives. He was useful too – opening my eyes to the natural world; a constant companion in our other life in the Highlands, leading me to otters and other beautiful creatures; soothing the children when calm reason was inadequate and he was also quite the hero.

One early-summer morning, we were woken by furious, urgent barking. Tina told me to go and see what was wrong.

'It'll be a fox.' I turned over. It was bloody 3.15 a.m. I still had thirty precious minutes of sleep left.

'No,' she said. '*Listen*. I've never heard him bark like that before.' I listened. Neither had I.

It was already light. There's a window on our landing and as I went down the stairs, I glanced into the garden. And yes, there was the reason for Maxwell's intense barking. There was a guy hauling his bounty – my bike – towards the fence. Fight or flight kicked in. As I ran down to the back door, Maxwell was waiting there. He was not impressed. He looked up at me as if to say, 'What the hell kept you? This is no fox.' He had metamorphosed into a wild animal and was raging like a wolf set to kill, his lips pulled back, incisors ready to rip the guy apart. It was a vignette of primal instincts – for both of us. I glanced at a wooden chair outside and decided that was how I was going to defend my family. I opened the door and we bolted out, both of us naked as the day we were born, barking and shouting. The imposter turned round and, seeing the two of us rushing towards him, dropped the bike and scrambled over the fence, his life intact but with an image that would hopefully haunt him to the grave.

As we went back inside I calmed Maxwell, talking to him all the time, and in the kitchen I laid out extra treats for him. I told Tina what had happened as I showered and dressed and when I left the house for work, fully clad, a patina of reason returned and I reflected on the beauty of Maxwell's actions. Maxwell, the softest, friendliest dog in the world, was our protector. We loved him, fed him, gave him shelter, warmth and exercise and in that twenty-second burst of action, he gave it all back. And there we were together – Maxwell and me. Brothers in arms.

Maxwell made me more zealous than ever in my passion for animal welfare, giving a roaring fire to my ever-present, ever-growing awareness. He was trusting, gentle and loyal – the very qualities being exploited and perverted in sublime animals like elephants, made to die for human vanity and to dance for human stupidity. Now aware that I was fighting for him too, I could also hear the noises of other things spiralling out of control, in spite of Maxwell or the love of my family. Any word of comfort or understanding was futile, any gentle suggestion I concentrate on the 'good things' was facile. I became psychologically unable to watch any nature programme because I couldn't, like the rest of them, gawp and gasp in awe at a beauty we were system-atically destroying. From upstairs, I heard that *Blue Planet* was remarkable.

The paradox was this. I felt it all much more because of Maxwell, but it was Maxwell who helped me through it. Maxwell was there when I was on cloud nine and he was there when I crashed and burned. His preternatural powers were a balm for the soul and he was the animal I could protect.

There were so many others to save. I began to feel ever more helpless, shocked by pictures of animal cruelty, internalising everything with an anguish I felt physically. Like the day I opened the paper and saw an orang-utan and her child – the closest mother–child bond in all of nature, seven years together, with just each other – driven from a burnt-out forest into a village. They had been captured by a mob, tied and bound and pelted with stones, the mother still holding and protecting her child with all her maternal magnificence. I was haunted for days. This was to me a sacrilege, not just a slight against some precious deity. Gods come and go, prophets are lauded beyond their merits, but this was a heinous debasement of the purest love; a bond of love honed over millions of years, the key to our survival. There was no remove; no barrier between me and the horror; no ability to step away emotionally. I initially assumed incidents like that were mercifully rare, but soon discovered they were anything but. And once I knew the horror was there, then it was everywhere and it became my duty to find it and let it smother me like I wanted to destroy myself too.

Soon after this, on a crisp Sunday in November, Maxwell in a deep sofa sleep after our morning walk on the common, I headed off into town with the children to the Somerset House skating rink. On the tube lay a discarded paper and I picked it up. As my woolly-hatted daughters sat swinging their legs, I read about thirty thousand elephants being poached in Africa every year to slake the demand for ivory trinkets in the Far East. Literally trinkets. Nonsense like toothpicks and the ultimate parody of art – miniature ivory elephants. That's where we'd arrived as a species. I'd had no idea of the enormity of it – the terrifying scale of it. There, on the Northern Line, I sat in sickened shock at the numbers and the motherless children – elephant families ripped apart, faces ripped apart, all driven by poverty, guided by criminal cartels, gilded by craftsmen. I thought of beautiful Echo and her family and felt sick. All those families destroyed, once sustained so powerfully by mutual love and support and now obliterated by human vanity. I looked at my children and as the tube north gradually filled with my fellow primates, I wanted to cry.

Back home I got on the computer and delved more and deeper into the unutterable hell of the ivory trade, wandering into the internet labyrinth of no return, and I found something so horrendous, the feeling of shame will never go away. It was a photo, underneath which lay the spine-chilling words: Wake Up Mummy. This single image was both a thumbnail of human monstrosity and a tragic symbol of the most ineffable love.

On the edge of a palm oil plantation in Sumatra, a family of adult pygmy elephants lay dead – poisoned like vermin, dying a long lingering agony. Beside the eldest female was the fourth family member, just a few weeks old, trying to wake up his mother. He was crying. He'd been nudging and pushing her, even as she lived, and in her final hours I imagined how she would have fought desperately to look after him, writhing in pain yet trying to reach him and touch him with her trunk, to feed and reassure him. And just before she lost consciousness, after the final convulsions of agony, she would have tried everything to respond to him. To make him know she loved him. And he was by her side, desperate for her to be there for him. To move, react, show him everything was okay. And to show her he loved her. Wake up Mummy.

He didn't understand what was happening and never would. After he was rescued, would he remember her? When she was dying, did she think of the danger he was in and how she could protect him no more and never again?

I sat at the computer trying to comprehend and staring, not for minutes but for more than an hour. Look what we've done now. I couldn't move from that place. Eventually I wandered downstairs like a zombie and showed everyone else the photo. But they were busy – homework, admin, music practice – and when I held up my phone with the urgency and disgust and despair I felt, they agreed it was awful and they couldn't look. But I couldn't not look. Whatever the true grim tragedy, my animal-loving family were able to find perspective, but I'd been taken hostage by the misery.

I slumped onto the sofa as hell closed in and shut my eyes. I could still see him there. Wake up Mummy. I could never un-see him trying to wake her up. My mind was sinking; floundering in gloom, my eyes tightly shut like a baby's. Someone was there in the room. I half opened my eyes and Maxwell was sitting on his hind legs, his ears back and tail wagging, not in his happy wag, but like it did when he was anxious. I was relieved he'd woken up from his slumbers and was there.

'Good boy,' I whispered and then retreated again into my quest for sleep; some respite care. I was drifting and then

I felt a nudge. I opened my eyes. He jumped up beside me, laid his head on my chest and stayed there, his warmth pressed on me like the comfort blanket I needed. Much like that first day when I held him, he was holding me and making me better. There were no caveats, no nuance. Just a special place where we could share our sentience.

He was so attuned to my mood. He could never know why I was feeling like I was but he understood on a far deeper level, ditching the need for any rambling explanation from me. He just felt it and wanted me to be better. Like Candy did when I was sad.

But whatever Maxwell told me and however better he made me feel, the world was still insane, its daily horrors were enveloping me and there was more hell than I ever would have imagined. The spiral into the vortex of reality continued and got every laser beam of my hyper-focus. I spotted a story about baby elephants ripped from their families in Zimbabwe and sold to Chinese zoos for tens of thousands of dollars to 'help conservation efforts'. Their mothers were coming as close as they could to the stockades and holding pens without being shot at, calling for them day and night. One evening, having been obsessed all day by a picture of a young bewildered elephant, standing alone and outside in a cramped, dark cage in a Chinese zoo, in the midst of the brutal Chinese winter, I rang up the Radio 5 Live Breakfast Show team demanding that this be our morning lead story, this utter outrage. The fact that this story wasn't right at the top of the world's news agenda, I shouted, just went to prove that people couldn't have known and if only they did, they might care.

I sent Mick on the news desk the link – this tiny elephant in a pathetic state of emotional starvation, yearning to be where he belonged. 'This has to be our lead story, Mick. This has to be,' I implored. 'The lucky ones will have died in transit.'

I could hear him listening politely. He expressed genuine horror at what I was describing. He too was outraged and horrified. In an effort that would have won him the Employee of the Year Award in Dealing with A Tricky Customer at the Call Centre Oscars, he explained why the stories we were doing tomorrow were more immediately relevant to our audience but that we should do a wider, more researched piece on the 'commodification of wildlife for commercial exploitation, trafficked between countries, testing to breaking point the limits of a rules-based system.'

His response may have sounded like a PDF file, but it did the trick.

'Okay,' I said. 'I understand. What are we leading on?'

'Ofsted.'

I felt people were ignoring the plight of elephants through lack of knowledge or lack of basic empathy. I had to make them see beyond the drab confines of their prosaic worlds and look at the elephants still breathing with their faces sliced off, not the charming ornaments on their mantelpieces and children's picture books. If Echo, like matriarchs across the elephant kingdom, did all she could to protect her family, I owed it to her, and believed I owed it to the world, to do all I could to protect her and the rest of her species.

I got to work and sent a blizzard of emails to TV controllers and commissioning editors, manically typed, badly copied and pasted and in a random variety of different fonts and sizes.

When one came back saying it was clearly a big issue and something I was passionate about but 'we did one last year and it didn't rate', it told me everything I really knew about our species. He might as well have said that he really wanted to buy an ivory mobile phone cover – the latest Chinese consumer monstrosity I'd chanced upon.

I needed to get more involved in the fight for nature. Over the years, I'd interviewed Will Travers from Born Free, an animal charity that campaigned across the world for wild animal welfare and conservation, so I rang him and bombarded him with more questions. Where is it safe for elephants? What about palm oil? How can we be so short-sighted? Why won't the Chinese government do something? People *eat* gorillas? People have gorilla-hand *ashtrays*? I fed him all the poison he already knew and he said it would be great if I could do whatever I could do. He looked so like his father, Bill Travers, who had played my screen literary hero Gavin Maxwell in the film of *Ring of Bright Water*, starring alongside Bill's mother, Virginia McKenna. Bill and Virginia had made the film *Born Free* too, the tale of Elsa the lioness. Will had grown up witnessing all the wonders of Eden while his parents were filming in Africa. But now Eden was being systematically destroyed tree by tree, leaf by leaf, tusk by tusk. His parents turned campaigners after all their magical experiences of the wild and the magnificence that for many of us seems like another planet. They founded the organisation Zoo Check (which later became the Born Free Foundation) after the premature death of an elephant, Pole Pole, in London Zoo. She had featured in one of their films but was now reduced to pacing up and down a tiny enclosure for the edification of London. There was a photograph of Bill and Virginia outside her enclosure and Pole Pole recognising them and reaching to touch Virginia's hand with her trunk. It was an unbearable but powerful image and, like so many I'd seen, a rallying cry for me.

Will and I went to meetings with politicians, civil servants and others to get them to put pressure on the Chinese and Vietnamese administrations, as well as to try to raise awareness and stump up some government money at home to help bolster the frontline battle of African nations being denuded of their natural heritage at an alarming rate. There is no nobler mission than saving another species. The message was gradually getting through, in no small part thanks to the support of William Hague. I talked to him in his office about the films and pictures: young tusk-less infants trying to wake their dead mothers. Something resonated with him deeply and there was real pain and anguish in his eyes; like with so many of us, it seemed to affect him at a very deep level.

Meetings could be dispiriting though. After one wasted half-hour with some uninspiring apparatchik – worse than a no-man, a maybe man – we stood in the House of Commons lobby. Will was staring into useless space and looked so despondent, with his dad's melancholy eyes.

'How do you stop yourself going mad, Will?' I asked him. 'All the stuff you see – what keeps you going?'

'Every time we get wins,' he said. 'Rescue a circus lion,

get a dolphin out of a Dubai millionaire's swimming pool . . .'

'But what stops you going completely mad?' I persisted. One of those 'asking for a friend' questions.

'How do you know I'm not?' he said and laughed, slightly.

I thought about what he'd said: 'we get wins'. That's important in life. We get hurt. We feel pain but we have love. Maxwell was a win for me every time I saw him because he restored my morale; my belief in the truth that somewhere, somehow, we would always have the beauty of our fellow creatures to cherish because there was one, at the heart of our family, giving us joy every moment he was alive.

I was also inspired by the work of the David Sheldrick Wildlife Trust in Kenya, the home of Echo and her family. Their work rescuing and rehabilitating elephant orphans, and eventually returning them to the wild, moved me deeply. There is no living form more stirring of something deep within us than a baby elephant. The DSWT was another organisation keeping my faith in our own species just about alive. The orphans' amazing, caring keepers fulfilled an unspoken promise to their long-lost mothers. There was a respect for life and a responsibility to the natural world that I believe is our moral, mandated duty. I told everyone I could about their work, wrote some music for their videos and made a speech at an event in London. But why didn't the whole world think like the people in that room?

Everything leads to a moment. I harangued away on social media, campaigned zealously, wrote articles for national newspapers, pouring my passion and rage onto any page I could find.

Off the back of the din I was making, I was invited to say something at the annual Global March for Elephants and Rhinos, which finished up in Parliament Square. Marching and congregating with a few hundred people who knew the despair and disbelief, who understood the outrage and wanted to fight back against the vile wanton destruction of the sublime in every sense, I felt at home, one of the family. I wasn't expecting to speak but the organiser of the march asked if I'd like to say a few words and offered me the microphone. I had nothing prepared but everything to say. Something happened. Electric surges were shooting through my body as I stepped onto the platform. Here I was, angry and real.

And out came my anger, sadness, frustration, fury; a eulogy for a species and elegy for its demise in one long raging roar – a torrential rant in the spring sunshine, spitting and spewing anger and despair into the putrid parliamentary air. I was soaring through my mind, picking off targets like the space invaders I used to play in the Aberdeen university union. I was unstoppable. Speaking in tongues, howling at moons. Raging at dying lights. Invincible. I pointed to the Houses of Parliament and vomited contempt for the charlatans; the callous self-interested merchants of murder and destruction who I imagined were all in on it, on the take, giving the corruption and crime gangs a free pass for a bit of soft power and genuflection to China, the Economic Emperor of the Universe. 'And I hope there are enough people in that place,' I screamed, jabbing my fingers at the House of Commons, 'enough people who can see what is happening.

A species is being destroyed. How can any of them live with themselves?'

There was an audible cheer at that from other gatherings at the jousting tournament of justice. Stop the War; Stop the Torture; Free Tibet; End Austerity. We couldn't all be right but we were. Some more so than others. The anti-war campaigners looked over in solidarity at my contempt for the elected ones. It might have been Iraq, Kashmir, Bedroom Tax or Jesus booming out of those speakers though it happened to be elephants. But they weren't my line of fire and as I caught sight of the tourists staring at our placards of blood and tusks, I spun round to face them. 'Are you listening?' I yelled. 'Are you *hearing* this?' Was I stereotyping? Yes. Was I scapegoating? Yes, but this was not exactly precision bombing. 'China, Vietnam. Stop the killing, yes you can,' I roared.

'Yes, yes, yes you can,' the crowd chanted back.

'Go back and tell your governments, your people . . .' I yelled at the selfie sticks.

The elephant marchers, actresses, and activists, campaigners, African heroes – these big-hearted, compassionate souls were listening to my every word. They had no choice. They listened and reacted. They cheered and applauded. Ten minutes later and I finished my distorted staccato diatribe and they cheered again. What else could they do?

Having dismounted the platform like I'd scored the winning goal, I was enthusiastically greeted by like-minded people who hadn't really expected what they'd just witnessed. I shook hands and back-patted, met some good people, and

I felt I'd done the most important thing in my life. I was no imposter. My sins were expiated. I was cleansed. Vindicated. Validated.

After a few hellos and goodbyes, I shimmied, stomped, slalomed through tourists like a Welsh fly half towards Westminster Underground station. Once on the tube I took a breath and found myself opposite a French-speaking family. A mother and two daughters.

'Vous êtes française?' I said in my best school French.

'Belgique,' said the mother. Her two children sat quietly looking at me through the tops of their eyes.

'Babar,' I said. 'L'elephant – sa mère etais morte dans la jungle pour l'ivoire et après ca tragedie – une vieille femme en Paris près de la Bois de Boulogne . . . um . . . adopted him.'

She looked at me with a mix of faint amusement and mild alarm.

'Ah, oui. Yes. I remember the children's book,' she said in accommodating English, so I'd please God never sully her mother tongue again.

'Yes,' I said. 'He was adopted. She gave him human clothes. Loved him and looked after him.' But the doors had opened into Green Park and they were gone. The sliding doors had shut.

As I trudged home, I felt an overwhelming tide of sadness and despair lapping all around me. Nothing was making me happy and everything felt out of proportion. I couldn't even be bothered to look over the litter on the common. Tina and the children were all out but as I rounded the corner, I thought about Maxwell, waiting for me by the door. And when he saw me, as it was every time I came through the front door, it was like he hadn't for thirty years. So much to tell me. So much to know. So much love to catch up on. I breathed out. There he was. Here was an animal no one was going to kill. My animal. No one would ever take him away. No one would ever harm him because I could protect him. I crumpled onto the sofa and within a second, he was up next to me and I felt his head on my chest and that feeling of warmth. One touch was enough. My head was just about back in the game. He gave me back to myself, my guide dog to serenity.

I had this urge to find out what had happened to the great matriarch, Echo, who'd led me to this moment. I picked up my phone and googled. Well into her seventies, she had lain down and died as the herd were making their way to some better place on an ancient migration route she'd learned from her own mother. She came and went and made the world better, in ways she could never understand, playing her dutiful, beautiful role in the great cycle of life until time ran out, just as it had for her mother, and her mother's mother, both of whom lived in her. She never forgot them as she came to the end: grandmother, daughter, sister, aunt. The herd moved on. They mourned and they never forgot but they moved on because survival depended on it. Maybe I needed to move on too. But to where?

A selfie with Davina, 2016

CHAPTER TEN

Long Lost Family

In 2009, my stint on *Watchdog*, a programme I had been presenting for nine years, came to an end. I'd loved being part of a team that exposed swindlers and had relished confronting conmen and even having the occasional bucket of unpleasantness thrown on me from an upstairs window. But the BBC wanted to change personnel; such is the way of the television world.

Watchdog was a one-off. I didn't think anything could ever match it. In some small, and often larger, ways, it had actually changed lives and had furthered my mission to rid the world of charlatans, poachers and pizza boxes. My working life was still a Piccadilly Circus in time-lapse: break-fast radio in London and Salford, TV current affairs debates and voiceover work, keeping ultra-busy because a minute to spare was not a minute to waste. New offers soon come round: a programme about motoring – just perfect for a man who hates driving – and some other foolery that involved self-assembly furniture, but TV office waste bins are stuffed with once-fabulous ideas.

When a call came about a meeting to discuss a programme that had been created in the Netherlands and was now a possibility in the UK, which aimed to reunite families – finding adopted children; finding birth parents; helping people find peace of mind, which, as I knew, was the hardest part by far – I was keen to know more. I'd worked with the production company before and knew of their high standards of care and compassion.

A few years earlier, I'd been the subject of their genealogy programme *Who Do You Think You Are?*, in a one-off adoption special exploring the balance of nature and nurture, and it had been a profoundly moving experience. We had concentrated on Dad's family of Scottish doctors, Australian emigration, the severe deafness that blighted my grandfather's life and which had shaped his relationship with Dad – and all the complex cause and effect of the story of what made the man who made me. Travelling to Brisbane, going to my grandfather's old school, meeting long-lost relatives' relatives, including – bizarrely – an eminent Australian archbishop, seeing the house where Dad's mother and father met as children, were all part of my emotional if not my actual DNA. And through it all I felt so close to Dad. In vivid dreams I could smell the shaving foam on his morning face as he lifted me up, kissed me and spun me round.

During the making of that programme, I'd uncovered something he'd never uttered a word about to any of us. During the war in Burma he'd fought in the brutal battle of Kohima – an event beyond description in its relentless unimaginable horror. When the military historian on the show explained to me how Dad's regiment had been part of it for days on end, it was hard to take in. Mum and Dad were devoted to each other, so it was a shock that my discovery was hers too. He had never, in all their years together, told her. Why would he? This was for him to know. Mum, and then Fiona and I, had given him such happiness, so why would he want to return to hell and take us with him? But in the dignity of his silence, something seemed to make sense. I was so proud of him and wept at what he'd been; and what he'd been through seemed to explain much. His tendency to worry and anxiously over-think things; his visceral aversion to violence, conflict and cruelty. There were clues. Clive James had a programme on a Sunday night with clips of an extreme and histrionic game show on Japanese TV that had a distinctly sadistic edge. When that segment came on Dad would just get up and leave the room, but not in a normal way. It was in his expression. He was unable to watch. And when I was about thirteen, I asked him about the war and he told me his well-worn jungle tales – a comical attempt to cross a river, or having to chain-smoke to burn the leeches off his skin. I once asked if he ever killed anyone. 'I don't know,' he said.

Our episode of *Who Do You Think You Are?* had been really well received and I was proud of the message that came across: that it is ultimately our parents' love that defines us, and not our genes. I'd filmed a sequence with Mum and Fiona and had said on camera how fortunate I was to have been adopted into my family. Mum had said – with no cue or script – how lucky she and Dad had felt too. After the show was broadcast, a whole host of people with a connec-tion to the world of adoption got in touch and when I was out and about, many others crossed the street, or spoke to me on the tube or tram to say what a positive message the programme had given out. And for me, Mum and Fiona, with Dad being so celebrated in the programme, it felt as though he was present in our lives again.

But it wasn't all positive. A few days after the broadcast, we were together in Mum's house and I opened *The Scotsman*, turning to the TV reviews to see if they'd written anything about the programme. The reviewer was raving about this compelling exploration of Dad's family tree. Simultaneously, he expressed absolute love for Dad and absolute loathing for me; what a wonderful story Dad's was, 'in spite of Nicky Campbell'. He went on to write that I was an annoying presence who unfortunately had to be a part of it, and the killer line, the headline, which perfectly summed up the tone of the piece, 'Grafted onto a fascinating family tree', knocked the breath out of me.

Mum asked me why I was upset and then had a quick read of it. She dismissed it all as the ranting of a 'nasty piece of work' and said what a marvellous reaction she'd had from all her friends and how well they thought I'd come over, but right then she could have produced a petition of an infinite number of people affirming the same thing and I'd still have believed the review. It was there in black and white. Once again, and as always, I was an imposter. I tried to ignore it, set it aside, bury it under the praise for Dad. But when someone points out your deepest fear, you know they must be right.

Five years after the film I made about Dad, and that review, and there I was wandering up endless flights of old wooden Soho stairs for a meeting about this new idea. I was excited for sure, but still concerned about the duty of care. I knew only too well how it could go, that the mothers and children and siblings that they were going to reunite weren't contestants on some reality TV show, where people step outside their 'comfort zone' and go on incredible 'journeys'. This was a programme about real reality, a journey into the very heart of who we are. Still, I knew the production company and I did like their proposed title. *Long Lost Family*. Who isn't lost at some time?

It didn't take me long to voice my concern. As we introduced ourselves, I said, 'If this isn't done right you can properly fuck things up.' There was a pause as everyone looked at me but then the entire process was explained, the levels of support to be provided, ranging from psychological tests, social workers and professional intermediaries legally able to access adoption files, to ongoing advice and thorough aftercare. It was to be exemplary, giving those who wished to be reunited with their relatives structure, guidance, realistic expectations and counselling. And the knowledge that they were not in this alone, that by sharing their intensely personal stories, they were inspiring others, part of something much bigger.

I had a lot to think about. This would be a huge personal challenge and I had to be prepared for that. All those inner conflicts, unresolved issues and mixed emotions stared back at me from the bathroom mirror.

I talked it over with Tina and together we watched the American pilot that the producers had given me, warning: 'It's very American, Nicky. Ignore the reunion oak tree on the hill and ignore the camera lingering on the presenters.'

The flim-flam notwithstanding, the heart of the concept of the show was deeply moving and important and it sealed my decision. A week later I met with the production and ITV teams and Davina in a busy hotel lobby with a coffee shop and bar. This was familiar but everyone was punctual. Davina has first-name fame and all my inner don't-deserve-to-be-there feelings were noisy and threatening. Within minutes I realised that she was warm, down to earth and, most importantly, that she completely got it.

If I'd felt this from my initial meeting, it was confirmed here. This wasn't a 'project' that would hopefully 'win the slot' and grab 'audience share'. The team would be headed by Ariel Bruce, one of the country's most experienced and admired social work professionals. And this wasn't about being a 'hello, welcome and thanks for joining us' presenter. In fact, this wasn't about presenting. It was about existing within it.

Once home I rang Mum and told her about the premise for the programme. The social worker in her asked about the ethics and the care and I outlined all I had digested from my meetings and talks with the production team, one on one. She was reassured, positive about my participation, and she said it sounded like a fine idea. By the end of our conversation, I was ready to confirm and commit, excited about what lay ahead. I was convinced that *Long Lost Family* had the potential to convey just what it was like being adopted: how we feel, how we explain it to ourselves and the struggle to work out who we are. It would also give insight into the mothers who had given up their children for adoption, all of us babies taken away and taken in while they endured a kind of half-life as they grieved for the living.

The contracts were signed and we were on our way. The programme was announced in the press and there was a small element of backchat – that this would be manipulative and insincere, exploiting people's deepest emotions for cheap TV. But they didn't know the people working on it. They didn't know the values and ethics at the heart of it. There was an exhaustive and meticulous process to pick the production, the camera and sound teams. Being good at your job was all very well but without empathy and emotional intelligence, you weren't going to be allowed anywhere near this terrain.

After we made the first programme for the decision-makers to see before the final-final green light, Peter Fincham, the ITV controller at the time, said that away from the raw emotion, the searches themselves were absorbing and fascinating; he wanted more emphasis on them, showing the viewers how we did it. And he was right. The people contacting the show had tried everything they could to find their relative, so the lateral thought and intuitive detective work of Ariel Bruce and her team gave the programme even greater depth.

Davina and I never appeared on screen together but when a reunion was in progress, our work was done – she having been looking after the searcher and me the found person. We would sometimes check in with each other over a sandwich and cup of tea in a local cafe or pub. Then it was as if reality had retuned; a decompression after being at the heart of the most extraordinary moment in people's lives. We were in a cafe in Lichfield after filming the first programme when I got a jolting reminder of the world of celebrity: a woman very politely came up to the two of us, asked for a selfie, gave me her mobile and stood beside Davina.

Very early on in the first series I met a birth mother in Shropshire. She was a kind warm woman in her early eighties and her son wanted to find her, to tell her not to worry, he'd had a great adoption and wonderful life and meeting her, the woman who gave him life, would make it complete. She had never thought and never dared think that this day would come and, when I gave her a letter he had written in case we found her, she asked me to read it to her. I tried. He expressed everything so well and I understood every word – the inner, yearning need to know who he was, or who else he was. As I read it she listened intently and then she noticed that I was crying and she leaned forward and put her arms round me to make me better. None of this made the cut, thank God, but it was then that I realised that I wouldn't just be meeting the lost and found in every episode, in some way, I'd be meeting myself and Stella. And thinking about Mum and Dad.

I began to meet mother after mother who, until they came to *Long Lost Family*, had searched and had been searched for in vain by the babies they'd last seen, in the most traumatic circumstances, decades before. It fell to me to explore their feelings and their reasons, creating an emotional intimacy that was extraordinary. We'd sometimes talk for two hours, during which the mother would take me to a fading memory that seemed like yesterday. I'd meet the young woman she was then, who would tell me about the worst day of her life – what it was like when he or she was taken from her arms; how she was left alone and then the car moved off. Being in those moments with these women could be unbearably raw and over and over again, I felt I was there. That it was me being taken away. Over and over and over again.

But everyone's story is so different. Some mothers seemed to have been able to brush themselves down and move on, even seeming matter-of-factly detached about what happened, as if they were talking about another woman, in a different lifetime, now another person. I came to understand that it wasn't just the adopted child who assumed a new identity, but also the birth mother. Her identity, however, wasn't a birthday present. It was born of the need to somehow survive the past intact, if not leave it behind, and then remove it from view. So many women referred to their younger self, as if she were someone else. Another kind of imposter, but one yearning for redemption.

They wanted to talk and yet, this moment came from such a faraway place, often in the context of having more children, a happy family, that it was jolting, hard to make sense of. 'It was all such a long time ago and very sad at the time,' she might say, 'but I was young, terribly naive. I just hope he's had a happy life. That would be wonderful to know.' And then, when I showed her a picture of a son or daughter, now and also when they were growing up, the world would stop. I'd see in her eyes the person she was

– a young woman's eyes, the truth of what this means in the moment and has always meant – and the still silence as she stared unblinkingly and then stared all over again. 'Can I keep this?' she'd ask.

Once in far-flung climes, I met a birth mother who'd emigrated, not just geographically but emotionally, and who, when contacted by the programme, felt she 'owed it to him.'

I had a photo of her son and gently handed it to her. 'He looks nice,' she said and placed it back on the table, but not as others did, in front of her so she could continue looking at him because that's all she'd ever wanted to do. No. She put it down and pushed it away like a playing card in a losing hand and then looked up, never looking down again. Never looking back. She had buried it so deeply. 'I had to,' she said, unasked.

But it's the desperate, whispered question that so many of these mothers ask in the eye of the storm that always stops me in my tracks. 'Does he resent me?' It's easy to explain that if he resented her, he wouldn't want to find her as much as he clearly shows he does by contacting *Long Lost Family*. 'No,' I tell them. 'He bears no ill-will.' But, even as I finish saying it, we both know it's not always that straightforward.

I see the young women they once were. And sometimes I even see the child in them – he or she is never far from the selves we use to navigate this strange world of grown-ups we all find ourselves in. Adulthood is a thin veneer. In their late sixties, twin sisters, Kathleen and Jennifer, were reunited. One had been completely unaware of the other's existence for her whole life. Davina and I stood on a hill in a park looking down at the empty white bandstand, beyond the piles of leaves, as these two ladies skipped towards each other like eight-year-olds. Just like when Esther and I took our socks off to compare toes, in my flat after we first met, and were like two excited children at the seaside.

After filming *Long Lost Family*, each and every episode, I found I was wiped out. It was all still alive and kicking inside me – it has been all my life – but when I got home, I too could go to that enchanted place called childhood again. Maxwell was always beautifully oblivious but wonderfully attentive. Here to play, and there was no better way to escape from being a grown-up and retreating to my true self than losing myself with him, comfort that is a million light years beyond words and beneath consciousness.

I was on my way to meet a birth son, now in his early forties, to tell him that his birth mother had been in touch with the programme and was looking for him. She had gone on to marry his birth father, so he also had four full siblings. We had told him that news off camera, as it was a hell of a thing to process, potentially magnifying any feelings of abandonment. But he understood, and saw nothing but joy in the situation.

Arriving at in the station late morning, I got the call to be in the middle carriage of the train as we drew in to the West Country. The crew would be at the end of the platform so they could film me getting off and walking along the edge of the train in sharp focus among the blurry throng. Then another couple of shots – one in close-up and one of my reflection in the station's window – and finally into the taxi, a few times from different angles, until we were on the road and heading for the adopted child, once known by another name. Just hours after being born, he was taken from his sixteen-year-old mother. She had changed and fed him, told him she loved him and that she never wanted this to happen, and then it happened. He was gone and a few hours later, he was someone else.

In the car I told his story to camera, wondering how he would feel about his birth mother wanting to meet him. This was her search, her yearning, calling out for him in her dreams. She and his sisters and brothers had wanted to find him for years, ever since she'd felt brave enough to tell them that she'd had a child with their father when they were young – too young – and had abided by her parents' wishes and given him up for adoption.

While we were filming the lead-up to our meeting the atmosphere, among the sound and camera man, the director and me, was, at least on the surface, jokey and chatty. This was not insouciance. Far from it. We knew the next couple of hours would, at times, be unbearably raw and there would be something that resonated at a deep level in all our lives. This wasn't someone talking about their dream house or holiday from hell. What we were about to watch this man experience was at the heart of who we are as human beings.

We were at his house. I knocked and he answered. Mid-forties, good-looking, upright guy, obviously confident but, understandably at this point, outwardly reticent. And as I knew, inwardly terrified. He was welcoming but not effusive, no doubt wondering if he'd made the right call to go through with this. I liked him and his partner instantly as we ate home-made cake and drank builder's tea. As the crew set up in the living room, we relaxed as we talked more. Always aware not to stray into the conversation we were bracing ourselves for, I wanted to calm his apprehension.

'This is mad, isn't it?' I said.

'Off the scale,' he replied and in all the years I'd been doing *Long Lost Family*, I'd never heard a better phrase to describe it all. So off the scale. So far beyond the normal realm of life.

'Did you ever trace your birth mother?' he asked, 'or did she ever trace you?'

'I traced her,' I said. 'A few years back now.'

'And did it work out?'

That unanswerable question – did it work out? I could have given him any number of answers and they'd all be true. It did and it didn't. It might do. It never will. It sorted me out and fucked me up. But in this moment, I wanted to tell him something that would reassure him – a safety net for high-wire expectations, but also something fundamentally true.

'I'm so glad it happened,' I said. 'Imagine never doing it? Being an old man and thinking what might have been.'

A voice called from the living room. We stood up and went next door to take our places on the sofa. It was bright and comfortable, looking out onto a garden where we could play on the trampoline if need be. 'Right,' said the director. 'We're ready.' On *Long Lost Family*, when the camera rolls the camera also disappears, the crew miraculously dissolving into nothing, and there are just the two of us. Two adopted children, talking.

I asked him how it had been finding out his birth mother had been looking for him and that he had four full siblings from his birth mother and birth father. 'Off the scale,' he repeated. None of the great authors I've never read could put it better. I asked him what his adoption had been like, and braced myself. Often there is a default position when the adopted person in front of me – and in front of themselves – say they could not have asked for better adoptive parents. But I can still see in their eyes that they feel it's something they should be saying; a sense of duty and also a need to believe it, that it is this which has sustained them and protected them. These are adopted children who feel grateful. But gratitude can be servile: I didn't really deserve this, but I was rescued, saved from purgatory and I'd like to thank the staff for looking after me so well. Our parents aren't staff. They are the parents of their children and we are their children. We are not grateful, we are thankful and those are completely different things. Not grateful to anyone, but thankful for everything.

But this man paid the most heartfelt tribute to his mum and dad. They were his mum and dad. 'They're amazing parents,' he said and I knew he meant it. His eyes were lost in a million happy family moments. He said it from the heart and it touched mine deeply.

Talking about his adoption was an affirmation of all of this – of my life, and his and the lives of so many more of us. He told me how, after he was adopted but before all the official paperwork had been completed, his father had taken the family on holiday to the coast, to celebrate this new life they had been given, and that this week, walking by the sea, sitting on the front watching the world go by, his new baby snuggled to him in a sling, had, for his father, remained the 'happiest week of his life'. His parents had loved him the minute they laid eyes on him and that alchemy of adoption meant that it was never meant to be any other way. His tears in telling me this were because he loved them, they loved him and they loved him so much that they were now completely behind him about meeting his birth mother. Unconquerable love.

I was often asked why, if people had a happy adoption, a happy secure childhood, they wanted to meet the birth mother who had given them away. I understood the question on one level – why put yourself through it – but unless you have been adopted, it is impossible to understand that yearning, earthed, need to know. Like me, like ninety nine per cent of all the other adopted people I'd ever spoken to, he wanted to know who he was, who she was and why she'd done the things she'd done. For as long as he'd known he was adopted, he'd always wondered. And the fact that he had the strength to do it publicly was because of his amazing family.

He expressed everything so movingly – his empathy for his birth mother and understanding of her impossible situation, the mind blowing excitement at meeting his full siblings. The backdrop and bedrock to everything was the strength and confidence to do this – to embrace it – and that was because his mum and dad loved him so much no mountain was too high.

There were long deep silences as he looked at photographs, thought about what it all meant and let it all flow through him. I felt every second. And then, when no more needed to be said, it was over. So intense had the last hour been that, with the subtlest change in body language, the spell was broken and we were out in the open. He looked exhausted but exhilarated and I was too, though also relieved. I sank into the luscious sofa and he looked again in disbelief at the photograph of his birth mother and siblings amidst the commotion and bustle of the crew dismantling the equipment. When viewers came to watch it on their telly screens, those who didn't understand might begin to, those who did might know themselves even better. Every day is a lesson.

Like so many people I'd met on *Long Lost Family*, he had no idea how much he helped me, what he showed me. The crew needed to film some more – shots of him with his partner, showing her photographs and telling her stuff, so much stuff. My day was done, but this would be a house full for a few hours yet.

Before we said our goodbyes, temporary brothers, long-lost babies, I said, 'When Davina tells your birth mother we've found you, imagine how she is going to feel.'

I saw him imagining it. Off the scale.

I left and hopped in a cab to the station, absolutely drained but with kids-at-Christmas excitement too. The best was yet to come – they would meet, they would understand and anything beyond that was what it was. Sitting on the train, after a session like that, I am never able to read, talk or be on the phone, or on the laptop. I just kind of *am*. This is not a job I can leave in the office, because it's all still alive and kicking inside me and it has been all my life. My conversation with him – more like a communion – had laid open some uncomfortable truths for me. His mother came looking for him and he was so accepting and embracing, while his real self or other self seemed to be utterly secure in his identity. He wasn't just accepting, he was sympathetic to his birth mother. He was a better man than me because he wasn't just a fine adopted son, which I hoped I had been, but he was a generous birth son, and in that I'd failed miserably.

There was only one conversation I was capable of having, because he would understand. When I came home to the usual merry mayhem, Maxwell got up on the sofa beside me and, sitting comfortably, put his paw on my leg like a helping hand. It was so human. Like he was pulling me towards him, wanting to make me better and never wanting to let me go. Happy again.

What if I'd had proper emotional and professional support? People to help, to talk to and to run to? I wondered what my reaction would have been if, like that man's birth mother, Stella had traced me. Then it wouldn't have been on my terms and I might have wondered what she'd wanted from me. And why now? But, I thought, maybe that way round I would have done everything in my power to protect my parents, rather than keep them away, and talked it through with them. Whatever way round though, I was coming to see that no, on a very basic level, it hadn't worked out. Stella didn't initially look for me, but then for the rest of her life she tried and for the rest of her life, I hid. My own shortcomings as a birth son were now more and more laid out bare to me.

Although Maxwell was always my soft landing, an escape to a better me – more basic, unaffected, unburdened, perhaps somewhere, actually, the truest me – the din of desperation got louder and louder. And no matter how much I was learning about myself from *Long Lost Family*, I obsessively, compulsively, began each day with a search for pictures or testimonies of cruelty to animals. I'd turn up for the breakfast show or filming on *Long Lost Family* with those stories of animal cruelty screaming in my head. Everyone's house we visited seemed to have baby elephant ornaments. One gentle birth mother in the west of Ireland had little figurines of dolphins on the wall and mantelpiece. My small talk to her before our proper conversation was about the dreadful dolphinariums and the annual dolphin drive in Japan that turns the sea blood-red, babies bobbing about helplessly looking for their mothers, mothers on their way to being processed as pet food. It hadn't been the best start to the day. I'd arrived at Colchester station to meet the crew, brandishing the picture of the baby elephant standing beside his dead mother in Borneo. It had been in the paper again, linked to a story about palm oil plantations, and I couldn't un-see it even when I opened my eyes the next morning. And yet, I was still just about functioning, even if increasingly I was hanging on by my fingertips. But then I let go and I fell.

The day started as they all had over the past few weeks. Half an hour before I went on air, I had logged on and scoured the world for the latest elephant news, a reflex action by now. About ten minutes before we went live, I'd found an awful caption and then dived further and deeper into the hell, because if I didn't, I was saving myself from myself; lying to myself; treating myself like a mollycoddled child, protected from the grimness of reality.

In those ten minutes of descent, I saw a headline in an Indian newspaper from just two hours previously, clicked the mouse in a cold panic and read about a family of elephants, most of which had been killed by a train hurtling at obscene and illegal speeds through the national forest reserve in the state of Kerala. The photographs were awful beyond words: the limp body of an adult almost dangling from a bridge and others lying nearby still achingly, sublimely beautiful, despite that unspeakable death. The remainder of the family group had attempted, as they always do, to revive their dead relatives and to stay by their bodies. Others in the herd had been driven away by sticks and firecrackers, but were still hanging around as closely as they could, looking for an opportunity to return and mourn. The matriarch was lost, most of the family were lost and the rest were lost without her.

At 6.30 I said good morning – the biggest lie I'd ever told – to our listeners. I felt sick in my heart – even more so than usual – and could barely breathe, but I was on national live radio fumbling for an autopilot, barely fit to fly. Rachel Burden, my radio other half and co-presenter, could always tell if I wasn't quite there, even if she didn't know where I had gone to, and had become adept at papering over the cracks before anyone saw them, and I was never more grateful to her that day for stepping in, even before I faltered.

It was futile. The poetry of simple love had been desecrated, the forest invaded by a deathly alien species and the destruction of Eden was a prophesy not a myth. I was teetering on the verge of proclaiming this to my interviewee from the National Federation of Builders, until some remnant of some other reality pulled me back.

I carried on, opening the microphone to interview politicians, speak to callers, foment debate and poke the hornets' nest, like I was playing the part of someone doing an impression of me. This was all broadcast muscle memory. It was all blah blah blah. An old hoofer whose legs had gone. I was weeping inside, racked by a pain worse than physical. I wanted to be someone else; somewhere else, but there was nowhere else that wasn't the same hell.

After the clock had agonisingly ticked round to the end of the programme, I made my way down Portland Place, stumbling along the Euston Road in a kind of zombie march. As I passed the old home of Capital Radio, all I could hear was Kenny Everett's voice, after my first stand-in shift back in 1986, when he'd told me, 'Don't be any good, "Nicky Campbell", or I shall have you garrotted and dragged down the Euston Road.'

And here I was, over thirty years later, garrotting and dragging myself, no need for anyone to do it for me. I crossed the road, narrowly avoiding a bus that swept round the corner from nowhere, a train in the forest. The driver sounded his furious horn. I couldn't believe the people all around me. I couldn't believe that everyone was blithely carrying on like replicants programmed to merely exist, while so much was going wrong in the world. I kept thinking about the fact that the rest of the family came back, trying to get near to the bodies to touch them one final time.

And I couldn't bear it. I couldn't bear anything so I gave up. I gave up in abject surrender to their indifference. Nobody cared. I was on my knees on the small patch of grass near the entrance to the station, my briefcase flung to one side, and I was sobbing with my hands cupped round my face. People walked, shuffled past, pushed past, feet all around set on an unchangeable course. Maybe they thought I was praying or drunk. Either way, best avoided, and so I lay there, crushed. I scrabbled in my pocket for the phone, rang Tina and through the mess of tears I babbled about what I'd seen that morning: a family, babies, mothers; bereft; slaughtered; Capital Radio; Kenny Everett; garrotted. 'Come home now,' she said. 'Get in a cab and come home now. We're going to sort this out. And while you are on your way home, I'm going to phone the doctor. The girls will be back later. Come home to us. Come home to Maxwell.'

I made it home. Tina had already organised for me to have time off work and made a doctor's appointment for the very next morning. The moment I started to realise that the way I was feeling and the things I'd been doing weren't actually normal behaviour was an epiphany. For some time now I'd been having random moments of crying when I was with trusted friends, family, on my own with Maxwell, when I just felt overwhelmed by a despair that seemed to come from nowhere – no specific trigger, but just a feeling that my heart was breaking.

Maxwell and Tina were the greatest reception committee ever. It was like they'd been planning my return together. His favourite toy at the time was a pig that made an awful honking squeal when squeezed. He picked it up in his soft mouth and as I embraced Tina, both of us in tears, he was shuffling round our feet sounding his klaxon, a medical dog making his way to the front of the cordon to give urgent attention to the patient. When Tina went to make tea, he unceremoniously jettisoned the pig, and in an instant swapped the manic excitement for a zen-like calm – a serene bedside manner, perfectly pitched. Like a dog sniffing drugs or finding someone under the snow, he just found my broken heart. A pack animal preternaturally attuned to the feelings of others, for were it to be any other way there would be no others. No future. No life.

That evening, the girls back from school, supper all together, I still had a hint of stubborn resistance to my plight. I'd be all right after a night's sleep. For heaven's sake – mental health problems and depression were terrible things that happened to other people. But I couldn't argue with Tina, who was resolute that I would be at that doctor's surgery the next morning, come hell or high water.

There was no messing around. My GP referred me to a psychiatrist, who saw me for regular assessments over the weeks ahead as he listened and took reams of notes that I tried to read but couldn't, upside down, with lines and words in different boxes joined up by arrows, sometimes pointing at bubbles, as he edged towards diagnosis and appropriate treatment. It was a kind of agony of self-revelation as I talked and we both listened. It's tough hearing yourself give voice to it all because you feel like a fool, like it's another person talking, and a part of you is rolling your eyes saying, 'get a grip, you weirdo.' Going out on the common, hiding behind cars and bushes, lying in wait for litter louts. Seriously? I told him everything, the obsessions, fixations, the manic missions, the terrible lows, deep depressions and despair.

His diagnosis a few sessions later was a big moment in my life but when he told me it was just a sentence. No fanfare. Just fact. I was 'clinically depressed and had bipolar type 2'.

'The Spike Milligan one?' I asked.

'Type 2,' he replied. 'He had type 1. It's a kind of mental epilepsy. Your high-wire adrenalin jobs help soak up the highs but the lows have just become too much to deal with. You internalised the cruelty you saw – took on the troubles of the world – and to an extent you always will, but you can and will be able to take a few steps back and get some perspective.'

Hearing this, knowing this, recognising it and having someone else telling me this, I felt a strange amalgam of validation and helplessness. He prescribed a drug that was used for epilepsy and bipolar disorder. 'You'll still be able to see the sunlight through the ceiling,' he said, 'but now there'll be a floor underneath you.' He swayed back in his dark green leather chair. 'Just out of interest,' he said, 'Has anyone else in your family been bipolar?'

'No,' I said, thinking of Mum and Dad. And then I realised what he meant by family.

Some of Stella's letters

CHAPTER ELEVEN

Dear Nicky

IT TURNED OUT Stella had lived with bipolar disorder in its most sporadically debilitating form for all her adult years. I thankfully avoided this, but we are what we are. The only challenge now I knew I too was bipolar was to make 'me' manageable, which seemed to be about keeping the best, controlling the bad, and so far so good. The medication played a massive part, but also my understanding of what I had, because knowledge is power. Recognising it for what it was meant the condition was no longer there to confuse, taunt and masquerade as normality. And finding out where it came from was another kind of empowerment.

I wasn't angry or resentful that I'd been burdened, or blessed. I was sanguine. This wasn't a curse; it wasn't a gift. It just was. Like brown hair or blue eyes. This was her legacy to me – my genetic inheritance. This was a watermark, not to mention irrefutable scientific proof. All our lives the adopted child dreams of knowing what someone who looks like them would look like. I'd never really seen myself in Stella but here was a resemblance far deeper than looks. And I understood more than ever before not just where I came from, but why. An episode of reckless abandon had led to the story of my life.

But as ever, I had to look both ways. This was a connection with her and maybe with those who begat those who begat her, but as well it was an inextricable bond that, in its intimacy, also stirred up all those adoption insecurities. For some reason I'd found it easier to dissociate myself from the womb whence I came than from this indelible stamp of Stella. I came from inside her and something of her was forever in me. Both essence and memento.

I asked Tina to tell Mum and Fiona about my diagnosis. I was, again, unwilling to talk to them about it more than in passing, because it emphasised my separateness; my not belonging. That adoption paradox will never die. We want to belong but we don't want that to mean we no longer belong. I didn't want Mum or my sister to be unsettled about my 'condition' and even subconsciously think – which I was sure they would – that I was so obviously different from them.

I told Esther, who took a keen interest in our mental matters and who established, through a friend in the business, and various research papers she read, that any predisposition for bipolar can be either mitigated or exacerbated by environment. I'd been lucky, raised in a benign environment – my secure, loving and supportive family. But this didn't fully spare me. Upsetting and traumatic experiences could, she told me, trigger it. And as for Stella, clearly any mistakes she'd made – ourselves included – made her bipolar worse so that even the smallest difficulty in her life could trigger it. As Tina had been advised before she bought Maxwell: always check out the temperament of the mother. Which mother though? My new one had changed the course of my life more than I'd ever thought.

Talking more to Esther, who had listened more carefully to Stella over the years, I listened more carefully to some of the things Stella had said to her. 'Some people,' she had once observed to Esther, 'are just more passionate than others,' and it struck me that passion – or maybe in our case surges of mania – came in many forms, one or two episodes of which had possibly led to our creation, which led to our adoption. And that it was that mania at its lower point, desperate for a way out, that had given me the impetus to find her. For Stella and me, bipolar was a biochemical thread, weaving its way through the narrative of our lives. Hers a hundred times worse than mine, but still I now had an insight, a different light.

I've met so many birth mothers on *Long Lost Family* who, without any of the mental health challenges Stella had, endured a lifetime of pain often best unacknowledged and who coped with it, or didn't, in very different ways. There was a mother who we had found for a son. In his early forties now, he wanted to meet her, before it was too late, to tell her everything had worked out. He wanted to tell her he'd had a good life; but as is sometimes the way, I sensed he was looking for something better, a desire to be loved more than in his heart of hearts he truly felt he had been.

She lived in New Zealand and I'd flown out for a head-exploding five days of filming. Those cross-planetary long-haul flights are a battering ram on the mental health and I arrived brittle and jangly. She was understated and seemed happy enough with life – forward-facing, breezy and optimistic. I asked her about meeting him again and she said she was looking forward to it, tremendously. The whole thing, she said, had been 'such a lovely surprise'. I looked at her, wondering if she was terrified – often a mother realises she won't just be seeing her child but also meeting her former self again – but she was giving nothing away. It was when I asked her how putting him up for adoption, having him taken away, affected her now that she dropped the bombshell. 'I haven't had a decent night's sleep in forty years,' she said and I was momentarily unmoored.

The next morning, on the way back to the airport, we dropped by her bungalow for a coffee. It was like suburban America there – no garden fences, just lawn and then cul-de-sac. The garden was immaculate, the birdsong alien and unrecognisable. No one in this neighbourhood knew the pleasant woman at number 23 had for years been lying awake before that strange dawn chorus. I rang the doorbell and there she was. She looked so different from yesterday, unburdened and decades younger. She told me she'd had her best night's sleep in years. The torment she'd been so good at suppressing was gone.

This is what we hide. These are the agonies we deal with. And it struck me that Stella's highs and lows meant that the long, aching pain might have been a torture.

In the outskirts of Auckland, that birth mother's knowledge and discovery that her baby was well and happy and wanted to meet her was a healing. I'd seen that healing, seen it happen before my very eyes so many times before. That feeling of earthly paradise that had lasted for a few days when she was with her baby forty-five years before was regained, and now she was ready to meet the man he'd become – and the young woman she once was.

You think, and think, and overthink. I flew out of Auckland that night, my head humming and whirring like the mid-ocean cabin I was in. The crew darted up and down the dusky aisles like shadows and I kept checking the time zones on my phone, trying to work out when was now. Yesterday I was on my way and now it was yesterday again. There was no escape from the past. I thought about the song 'Yesterday Once More', in which nostalgia feels more like an enduring loss. At the best of times Karen Carpenter could give even the jauntiest ditty a deep melancholy, a yearning for something lost. Like the birth mother I'd met, smiling on one level, absolutely sincerely because life was okay, but on a deeper level, crushed. For forty-five years, she'd been escaping the relentlessness tyranny of yesterday. Maybe tonight, she would have yet another mercifully untroubled night's sleep. My thoughts were becoming misshapen, disjointed as sleep beckoned, but then as I was falling, I rumbled it and straightened myself. Did Stella sleep well in the days, weeks, months, years after meeting me? Did the night set her free? I never asked. I didn't know. She used to phone late at night and want to talk and talk, so maybe not.

It was a month since I'd met the birth son in the West

Country, a different *Long Lost Family* story. I'd envied his ability to accept and embrace his birth mother and yet hold on to the unassailable integrity and togetherness of his adoptive family. His birth mother had stretched her hand out and he'd clasped it tenderly. He'd tried to understand and when they met, he was there for her. And now, would always be. But he was also, fiercely, his parents' son. He always would be. What a great birth son. What a great son. A far better man than me.

I was six miles high above the clouds but beginning to plummet into the doldrums. I hadn't taken my meds because it was hard to work out when, and how many I'd had over the last four days of contorted time, clocks melting all over the place. The steward saw I was awake and asked if he could get me anything. I went for a different type of medication. When he came back through the cabin gloom, he placed the gin on my tray table with a little dish of nuts, and then knelt beside me and asked if I'd been in New Zealand filming *Long Lost Family*. I knew what was coming and I didn't mind. Everyone has their own story. All are interesting and some are more interesting than others. Adopted, after years of trying on his own, with the help of social services, eventually he'd traced his birth mother. But while his dream had come true, his dream was not the same as hers. She wasn't interested in seeing him. 'It was like being rejected twice,' he said. 'I just wanted to meet her and find out who I was, get a sense of my identity.'

I'd have felt awful for him at the best of times and right now I was struggling for something reassuring to tell him. But what? What could I possibly say, other than suggesting, weakly, that he was probably best off without having met her if that was her attitude? But I knew that not to be true. We all need to know where we have come from and until we do, we are incomplete. The pilot's voice came over the speakers, warning of turbulence, and the steward immediately snapped to attention, checking my seat belt and moving on. Turbulence. Fucking right, I thought. She wasn't interested.

When we landed my flight-crew brother-in-adoption was at the door with a female colleague, thanking us one by one. He was back to his inscrutable professional self, as if his whispered confession in the dead of the night had never happened. He was back on remote. 'Thank you Mr Campbell,' he said and I wanted to hug him, comfort the lost – and rejected – child. But I was tired; vulnerable and vinegary. And it wouldn't have made any difference.

Back home and, hugging me, Tina told me never to go away again, as she always does when I come home from afar. And Maxwell was tugging my jacket. 'He's been spending a lot of his time at the bottom of the stairs,' she told me. 'He's been rushing from room to room, realising you weren't there, coming back downstairs and whining.' I reached down and buried my face in his neck. I still smelt of plane but he smelt of home.

I'd arrived back in time for the school day; yesterday, today or tomorrow. The house was faster than a silent film – grab-a-bag, kiss-a-mum, hug-a-dog, out the door. I had to sleep. Maxwell leapt up onto the bed because he knew I'd let him get away with it. It was the best I'd slept in forty hours. The next thing I knew it was 2 p.m. and the next thing after that it was late afternoon. My face was being licked. The home-from-school sounds were coming from the hall, so I stumbled down in my dressing gown with the boy in tow and sat for a while.

But I couldn't engage. When I'm tired, the record never fades and today's track was the air steward: 'she wasn't interested', as verse and chorus. The needle was stuck. And the expression I'd seen flash through his eyes as he told me. I'd looked away but now it was all I could see. It had showed me what I was. I'd been a terrible birth son. He'd have given anything to meet a dishevelled woman, half conked out by sleeping tablets, struggling for coherence and courage. He'd have given anything for that. Imagine if he'd knelt beside me and said, 'I met my birth mother because I wanted to get a sense of identity and after I met her I couldn't really be bothered with her because she didn't live up to my expectations.' What would I have thought of him? How would I have felt if Stella hadn't been interested? Like him – a double abandonment.

They say stay up, go with the jet lag, but I hadn't. By 10 p.m., everyone else in bed, I sat on the sofa with my hand on Maxwell's head and I let it come, a reckoning. My adoption search had been all about who I was, a mountain echo. Who am I. Am I. Am I. I'd never bothered addressing the question who was *she*? Who was Stella? Since I met her in 1991, I'd fostered this negative impression of her maybe as far removed from reality as the idealised one I'd constructed when I was growing up. The perfect mother, in all but motherhood, had become a bothersome stranger I couldn't be bothered to know.

Maxwell was snuggling and snoring, his paw on my leg. I thought about the first question Stella had asked me. Do you like dogs? What a *brilliant* question that was. My life was spent asking questions, the perfect vocation when you've got no answers, and it hit me what an instantaneous, wise and incisive way that was to assess someone's character, not foolproof perhaps but pretty good. A psychometric *coup de grâce.* I mean, if someone said no in both Stella's world and in mine, they'd have some serious explaining to do.

What kind of person would say no? Someone averse to love, loyalty, fidelity, attachment, gentleness. Someone with no curiosity or sense of wonder. It's a test of humanity because loving animals means we understand ourselves. Those who love animals are the best of us and we don't buy the desperate needy lie that it's all about us. Dogs – and cats – are emissaries from the animal kingdom. Through them we see the wondrous and sublime possibilities and realities of the world beyond us – not above us. And as an opening question to her son and later, daughter, who she had not seen since a few days after giving birth to them, it was a totally on-point question. Esther had told me that Stella had told her, several times, that she, Stella, was a shrewd judge of character. Maybe she didn't make the right choices in life, had a disastrous marriage, but that didn't mean she wasn't a shrewd judge of character.

Her question about dogs was also about her and me, about Toby scuttling about under my cot to guard me. Our mutual best friend. She'd grown up on a farm. She knew how dogs take us to a better us and give us back to ourselves.

I looked down at Maxwell and I heard the refrain strike back up and I knew what I needed to do.

A few weeks back, searching for some papers, I'd come across the letters that Stella had sent me, the ones I had kept. I'd never read them. I'd never even opened them. I hadn't been interested. I felt a cold shiver of self-loathing and failure. I'd do it now. Maxwell was there for moral support. I went upstairs to get them, Maxwell following me up and then back down, as if he was part of the mission. Or a guardian angel.

I was ready but I was petrified, just like those unopened envelopes were petrified in time. Stella might be scared too, because it was like we were meeting again, but this time it was me who was late. Thirty years late. I was the one whose head was messed up.

A good birth son would have kept them, treasured and cherished, in a wooden box he got for Christmas. I kept them in a dusty box file held together by masking tape containing life's flotsam and jetsam. A backstage pass for a Paul McCartney concert, a photo of me and Mick Jagger from 1991, photocopied newspaper cuttings, letters on headed notepaper with no email addresses, old diaries with entries like 'Dentist 10.45.' Going decades back. And a decree nisi on parchment.

As I opened the first envelope, the glue miraculously still holding, I wondered what these letters would reveal. I remembered the handwriting. Illegible, as far from a confident flourish as one could get. Small, spidery, tentative and defensive, each word taking time and effort to decipher,

194

like inscriptions on gravestones in old churchyards. I could do this, but slowly – working it out, reading it in, reading it out, taking it in.

All those years ago the handwriting had been a barbed-wire fence, but also a get-out clause allowing me the excuse not to bother reading. The two or three I had read, and discarded, had sapped all my energy, the effort inversely proportional to the reward, and at the end of every sentence I'd been pleading for parole. But now I had all the time in the world, whatever time it was anywhere in the world.

It wasn't as if I was looking for any great revelation, but I was now alert and interested. Maybe there would be something glinting, just as there was when I met her, that moment that had stayed with me, when she leaned back to look at me and a younger woman appeared, with a sense of wonder for the craziness of life. The moment when she'd moved from the safety of platitudes and banality to something real. Maybe she was here in the letters. In a secret code. Secret messages to her long-lost son. A message in a letter.

I was now taking out a letter dated 14 December 1990. I thought of the air steward. Opening that envelope would have been a defining moment in his life. I hadn't even granted it the luxury of the light. Ungrateful child.

I opened the first one and then the second and then the rest, as if I were opening my A level results. Quick quick slow. And there they were – unedited torrents of thought, reams and streams of consciousness, all in her microscopic-hieroglyphic scrawl. Words needing to be written but strangely reluctant to be read.

Dear Nicky. Dear Nicky. Dear Nicky. Normally that greeting at the top of a letter is meaningless – nobody who writes them thinks the recipient is dear to them. How did that happen? But here the word hit me as real. She used the word through the letters too: my dear, well my dear, my dear Nicky. Dear after thirty years and this was the first thing that hit me. She was in her life respectable and irreproachable, but there was so much more under the surface. In that one word and in her whole life, I was dear to her.

The letters lay in front of me and now, bare and there, they seemed so significant, such an intimate way of connecting. You don't just bash out a letter and press send; as the different dates within the same letter indicated, you take the time to think, write, compose and really say things for now and for all time. Keepsakes forsaken. But they were there. I'd lived at four different addresses since I'd received them but they made it all the way. I'd taken them from the marital home after getting divorced, with my clothes, books and music. Then I took them again and then I took them again. I could have left those letters with all the other stuff along the way, in a drawer in a chest for someone else to find in a junk shop. But you don't do that. That would have been wrong. This wasn't junk. This was the woman who gave birth to me. Maybe I knew that someday this moment would come. I thought about that and hated myself slightly less.

Each letter began with the hope that I was well. And then a flicker of unexpressed despair, an intimate explanation as to why I hadn't written back or phoned her, as if she was clarifying my lack of good manners to a third party: I must be tired after my trip to New York; I must be exhausted after working so hard; I was so busy at the moment. 'I know your diary is well booked up,' she told us both. 'Please write to me when you can.' 'Please phone me when you can.'

Thirty years later and the excuses had dried up. She was my birth mother. I'd surely owed her more. I read on. Always giving me the benefit of the doubt, she had so clearly wanted to see the best in me, project the best on to me: an idyllic marriage, a glamorous career, a son who she hoped would have her to stay. She devised the propaganda, how she wanted it to be, constantly concerned for my well-being, on the roadshows, on my travels, in my life. And before we met? There's a fleeting reference. She 'often wondered' about me and 'prayed' I was having a happy life.

I read on through 1990, into 1991, 1992. She was trying so hard to be a part of my life, to share in what she could. There were letters full of comments about my late-night radio show – the interviews, my choice of records, my midnight chats with listeners, which she thought I enjoyed. Her intuition there was right. I'd felt happy and relaxed talking in the dark, a confessional intimacy with strangers, sharing myself and reaching out. I'd never known until this moment that she'd been there, tuned in, listening to me. I'd been talking to her too. Just as I'd been talking directly to the person on the number 33 bus on their way home late at night, I'd been talking to the retired nurse in her sheltered housing apartment in Dublin who met her long-lost family and then kind of lost them again. And now here she was talking back to me, making points, comments, expressing opinions, sometimes very opinionated ones. Trying to reach me.

She wrote about her late brother, John, a lot. His achievements as a cyclist and a posthumous ceremony celebrating his life in that world. She missed him terribly and her pain was easy to read, in between the lines. There were the names and vocations of mysterious relations and people here and there who I had to meet and who really wanted to meet me, when I came over. A niece did this and was hoping to do that, while a cousin was studying hard and her brother was doing very well at school. She was inviting me in. Meet the Lackeys. And though they were just names on a page I could barely read, she wrote as if they were a line of guests welcoming me into the family. I'm sure, like me, they were far more interested in their own lives, but that's not how Stella wanted it to be. If I belonged to them I'd belong to her.

When I'd received these letters, together with the phone calls, they felt like a tsunami of irrelevance and vacuity. I'd told myself I had no time or energy to unravel the words and crack the code. I'd handed the phone to others, I'd stuffed the letters, unopened, into drawers. This is what I'd told myself then and this is what I'd told myself and others whenever I told them anything about Stella. But, now, the letters spread around me, Maxwell by my side, I was coming through the jet lag. This was about much, much more than not having time.

From the story of my creation as told to me by my mum; my stubborn withholding and then torrent of disclosure of my adoption; to the searching and finding of my birth mother;

to when I had met Stella in Dublin, in all the detail and projection and sharing in these letters, there was something missing. The thing that I now realised, had always somewhere realised, I'd been searching for all my life, listened for, looked for, but ultimately been too terrified I'd never hear.

On *Long Lost Family*, I'd spoken to so many birth mothers and even in the most defensive and closed off, there was always *something* – some suggestion of something deeper – or an acknowledgment of why there wasn't. A self-awareness. An explanation. Not for Stella though. Not in Dublin. Not in the telephone conversations. And now, late into the night, the ghosts still haunting me, not, it appeared, in these letters, letters sometimes written over days. Just a tiny scrap of a hint I'd wanted so desperately to hear her say what others had said to me: that she'd never wanted to give me up. That she'd had to bury it all. That she'd thought about me every day. That she'd thought about me on my birthday. That after we met, she'd said she felt years younger. That she was sleeping at last. That now she'd found me, she was never going to let me go.

But if she'd said any of this, I'd have screamed and run a million miles. I wanted to hear it, but it was the last thing I wanted to hear. It was at the heart of me but it wasn't me. The imposter's life, not mine. This was, is and always will be the paradox of so many adopted people. Better not to know then? 'Avoid the bother', as one adopted friend said to me, explaining his visceral aversion to ever tracing his birth parents.

The last thing I ever wanted to do was reject Mum and Dad. After I told her that I was tracing my birth mother, her well-intentioned but desperately sad words, 'we've been so lucky to have had you for twenty-nine years' were indelibly etched in my mind. Even to this day, it's unbearable to think about. It was as if my mum had been expecting Stella to take me back. Mum's glass was famously half full, but not then, and I'd carried that with me, I realised, until now.

Others had shown me the way. A TV show that changed the lives of so many and had changed mine. So many people were able to look both ways and for the adopted son in the West Country with the parents he loved with all his heart, he not only accepted his birth mother with joy, it was his parents' lifelong love for him that gave him the strength and self-confidence to do it. I remembered something else Mum once said to me: we share far too much as a family for anything to ever come between us.

I sat back on the sofa with my legs on the footstool and took some time out of the soul-searching. It felt like coming out of the deep end for air. There should have been a grandfather clock ticking and fire crackling; but I had the warmth of Maxwell and his slow slumbering metronomic heartbeat – warm and steady as my hand that stroked his head for comfort. I couldn't have done this without him. Just having him next to me meant that everything would be okay. That I could do this.

I'd been so unable, so unwilling to accept her lack of explanation, her lack of expressed regret, and now it was my turn, my responsibility as her birth son to try to understand why she was the way she was and what she really was beyond the shallows. Maybe it was this. That we – Deirdre and Nicholas – were the people from nowhere, the living dead. She'd had a lifetime of pain and disappointment. Why should she confront it? Why meet it head on? Take the line of least resistance. Only some kind of emotional masochist would watch that film again and again. By the time we arrived, it was too late. She'd wiped the tapes completely.

Or had she?

I took a deep breath. I had all the time in the world. I sorted the letters into a pile, steadied myself and began to read them all again, even closer, a mental magnifying glass, looking for more.

Two hours later and I found it. 'All the people who matter know about you,' she wrote. 'I have talked my life through to a psychiatric sister here. She is a wonderful help and I feel so much better since.'

I hadn't taken that in first time. It had been hidden in the undergrowth. But there it was – the shame but the steely determination, the courage to tell people who had never known and would never have imagined this woman would have had secret children. She told the 'people who mattered'. That included the entire network of relatives doing this, that and the other and God knows what else. She thought it was the right thing to do, because she did it. They might think badly of her; they would certainly see her completely differently, but it was the right thing to do.

I was done with searching. I sat back. I could hear her voice, her soft lilt. I thought again about our first meeting, running through the things she had actually said that had allowed us to connect. Our love of dogs, my love of music, her love of poetry. She'd mentioned one poem in particular – Yeats's 'The Wild Swans at Coole'. I'd never bothered to read it but I found I wanted to now, to understand why she had been so specific. I googled it.

The setting hit me immediately. I could smell the reeds and feel the cool of the water, the power of the 'bell-beat' wings and the joy of being a swan, the joy of just being; but at the same time I could feel the sadness, a yearning, an unsettling sense of impermanence.

As I read the last two stanzas, I understood. They swam, swan by swan. Each having its own companion. Fifty-nine swans. But why fifty-nine? Though unsaid, one was gone, taken or missing, lost or flown. Elsewhere. Never to return to the one to whom they belonged.

This poem meant so much to her that she mentioned it minutes into our first meeting, one of the first things she, Stella Margaret Lackey, had said to me. This poem was the bell-beat of her heart.

This was her letter.

Sometimes you don't need to talk.

CHAPTER TWELVE

All My Family

WHEN WE DON'T know, we imagine all sorts of terrible things. When we do know, we create our own immutable truths. For all these years I have thought – and held on to – the belief that Stella had nothing to offer but vacuous platitudes, precious little else but a neediness I didn't need. And so these letters have been a revelation. Not just because I've now heard more clearly some of what my birth mother was trying to tell me, listened and understood some of what she left unsaid, but because I've come to see her more for the woman she was and the choices she made. For so long, this lack of knowing – and my refusal to know – has been the hardest part of being me.

'All the people who matter know about you.' As far as I'd known, she had only ever told her sister, and possibly her brother, about Esther and me. Candour elsewhere would have come with too high a price – I'd thought – and was sure to open the door to unrelenting condemnation. A sign of the times combined with Stella's own internal sanctioning. But these eight words have made a big difference to me – an acceptance, however late on, that to her and to others in her life, I *existed*. She had not rejected me outright. She had not forgotten or forsaken me.

And while I may not have all the answers, will never get to ask the questions I would now have the courage and willingness to ask and keep gently asking her, I have, in her words, as much of an explanation as I'm ever going to get. And it's enough. After a lifetime of imagining her, meeting her and then turning away from her, having now heard a little of what she might, in different circumstances, have been able to tell me and maybe even have expanded on, she is no longer a one-dimensional character in my own psychodrama, no longer just a means to an end, the end being my right to know who she was. Now I know who she was in a much more profound and meaningful sense. She too exists for me.

My birth father too. He, who, still alive to life itself, loves to talk politics, about his horse, his dog, his visits to the pub, how Ireland really is. He's good at listening, good at talking, good at asking questions and good at honesty. An interesting, interested man, made all the more fascinating to me by the experience of going over to rural Ireland and having pints of Guinness in a pub that would make any Hollywood location director yelp with excitement: the locals with faces like character actors, a swear box by the till, the landlady a strict but tender matriarch.

'Don't grow up,' he once told me. 'That's the biggest mistake you'll ever make.' A fleeting glimpse of how he'd created his own walls, how he'd written his own terms and conditions. When we do talk, after however long, it's like it was yesterday since our last conversation, and I love to hear the Irish romantic and idealiser in him, as much as the realist, unsparing on the follies of the world, his own included.

And I don't need or expect explanations. He was twenty-three and she was thirty-six. I think of myself at twenty-three, unprepared for much, let alone for paternal responsibility, and then add the condemnation of society, the age difference, the iron curtain of religious difference, the marital impossibilities and the singular nature of the relationship. Had he been a man of her own age, maybe I would have judged him differently, maybe expected a bit of curiosity and a dashing of regret. So when he told me, 'I sometimes thought about you right enough' that was good enough. Often means now and again, which is plenty. And when I met him, he had a family, other children. He is my birth father, but somebody else's dad. Because of him, I was given life and because of him, I was given the man I called Dad, my real father, the finest man I've ever known.

It may have taken a while and it may have been a bumpy ride, but I have reached the point where I recognise my birth mother and my birth father for what they are and who they are. I am part of them and they are part of me. Two people who, in making a 'mistake', brought me into this world, for which, and to whom, I will always be thankful.

Family comes in myriad shapes, colours and manifestations and, as so many people on *Long Lost Family* have shown me, not just in their curiosity, but in their openness and generosity, that's nothing to fear. We can share in a part of a family and be a part of it on different levels and in so many different ways. It needn't even be complicated or oppressive, doesn't have to be alienating or denied. It's just a part of life, of who we are.

A magical childhood, itself a womb we both occupied; I share something wonderful beyond words with Fiona that no one else can ever fully understand; just as I share something extraordinary with Esther that no one else can fully understand. And my mum and dad – my adoptive mother and father, who brought me into the world, in the truest sense, a world into which I was welcomed. Their world became my world and to this day nothing reminds me of that more than seeing myself as a child, on the hillside where our family Highland cottage stood, gazing at the spectacular view down the glen to the mountains of the west and the loch below, breathing in the lingering smell of the soft evening breeze, watching my dad strimming the weeds, his pipe in his mouth, serenely happy. It was my job to call him in for supper. At the end of one blissful summer's day that seemed to be endless, like all those days, I watched him a while and then yelled to him and he looked up at me, smiling, the darkening waters of the loch in the glen below. I was so much a part of his happiness that nothing on earth made me feel like I belonged to him more than in those moments.

But belonging in the moment is one thing. Belonging all the time – and knowing to whom – is another. When you've been abandoned by the person to whom you irrefutably once belonged, knowing where you belong in yourself is quite another. You can drive yourself mad sifting through the relative scale of belonging: I belong to my parents but it was only because of Ronnie Cameron's presence of mind that they even knew about me; if he hadn't been their GP who would I have belonged to? What if the weeks in the babies' nursing home had turned into months, years? What if no one had come for me? I would have belonged to no one, not even my brief past. And if another Mum and Dad had come for me, would I have belonged to this version of myself . . . and so on. In the dark-blue moments, the contempt you feel for yourself for being unworthy of your birth mother's love, of being forced to belong to others, of being on the precipice of being abandoned and never rescued into belonging, can be the bleakest moments of all.

It's taken a while, but I know now that I can belong exactly where I want to belong, that nothing can threaten the integrity of that. I belong to my parents and I belong in a different way to Stella and, in different ways again, to my birth father. And mostly, I belong to myself in the truest version of who I am. Having that agency is an empowering lesson for any adopted child and that's what we always are and always will be – adopted children. Right from that moment of exchange, frozen in a time we can't even remember but will never forget.

Whether we have met or not, know everything or know nothing, we adopted children understand so much about each other on an instinctive level that we can never be total strangers. Like the family of adopted children I've met through *Long Lost Family*, we intuitively know that we understand so much about each other. I ask a question and I so often know what the other person is about to say and so often too, they read my mind. It's simple but mysterious, like playing snap with tarot cards. On one level it's a deep psychological and emotional connection, on another a lifelong play-date.

There's a look, a knowing glance, a tacit understanding of things only we can know; we're bonded because so many of our feelings and experiences are shared. For most of my life, knowing I was adopted and being known as being adopted gave me a feeling of aching vulnerability, but now it's a sense of solidarity, of belonging. And while I once yearned not to be an adopted child, now I wouldn't change it. Mum used to tell me that I was chosen, which was tantamount to telling me that I was different, and after a lifetime of living up to that billing, I'm so over it. Or at least so through the worst of it.

Being able to come to terms with myself has cleared my vision and allowed me to see that Stella was a far more interesting and rounded human being than I let myself believe. Far more than either the mother of fantasy, or the birth mother of anticlimax, both caricatures. Life is far more complicated. Her courage in meeting me twenty-nine years after she left me and in – eventually – telling her family about me was that very same strength that made her capable of leaving me for a better life. Strong enough to break her own heart. And now I understand, I understand, and I will forever be grateful for that love.

In a faded brown envelope in that dusty box file containing her unopened letters, I found her death notice, sent to me by my ever-solicitous cousin Robert. On receiving it I'd glance-read it, but the words had just been words and that was all; just stuff written because it needed to be written. It was different now though.

> *LACKEY, Stella Margaret (Dublin and Soran, Ballinalee)*
> *– September 14, 2008, at St Vincent's University Hospital,*
> *late Matron of the Royal Hospital, Donnybrook and*
> *Simpson's Hospital, Dundrum, loved mother of Nicky*
> *and Esther. Sister of Patricia, Willie and her late loved*
> *brother John; will be missed by her family, grand-*
> *children, sisters-in-law, nephews, nieces and friends.*

Missed by her family. I was one of her family because we had come home to her at last. And yes, she was a mother, a 'loved mother of Nicky and Esther'. She had been loved by me in the purest way, when she was all I knew and I was hers for just a short while; that time as momentous as any in a lifetime. 'We are,' wrote Carl Sagan, 'like butterflies who flutter for a day and think it's for ever.' Well, that was for ever. At that point in time, during those nine days that changed our worlds, I needed her and in those nine days, I always will.

And now, with the long view, I can see that when she made that heart-rending decision, she ultimately gave life to my daughters – Breagha, Lilla, Kirsty and Isla – forces of nature, singing their way through life, bubbling with love and loyalty, kindness and compassion; taking no prisoners, suffering no fools but caring for people and the planet. My daughters, my children – who wouldn't exist, if Stella hadn't done the right thing for me and my life.

Tina feels a physical pain when they're unhappy, their sadness calling at her heart like a baby's cry. I once asked her what it would be like, if as Stella had done, she'd had to give up two children, within eighteen months. She said it would be a physical pain 'so unbearable and life-lasting' that she was not sure she personally would have survived it. But if she had made it through, then, she said, she might have been able to function day by day on one level – live, work, laugh and love – but such a core part of her would be dead, it would like going through the motions. When Esther once asked Stella if she'd breastfed her, Stella shot back: 'Now, why would I want to do that' and that response always jarred. Stella dismissed the option as if it were the most ridiculous thing she'd ever heard, but beneath the ridicule there must have been torment. But I realise now that this ultimate-intimate, sensual mother–baby bond would have been another dagger in her heart, an attachment too far. That bond Tina feels and felt is visceral and umbilical. I'll never know nor possibly understand the ineffable primal might of that feeling – it's there in nature, in tooth and claw; but to think that Stella may have felt that way about me is both painful and humbling.

According to the primatologist Jane Goodall, chimps, our closest kin, are us without the fuss, and they tell science so much about the origins and instincts of human beings. In the immensity of time, our long-lost family are more like us than we are, because they reveal this essence that we've camouflaged, of our inner chimp. Jane has observed in wild chimps every kind of mother – wonderful, terrible, mediocre, mothers who couldn't cope, mothers who helped others, mothers who looked after orphans – and in this, she believes, they are so like us. Complex and unpredictable.

It's not straightforward being a mother, not just instinct and add water. My birth mother couldn't be my mother beyond giving birth to me. But she wanted me enough to give birth to me. And my adoptive mother wanted me and, despite not having carried me, harboured that deepest desire to love and cherish. It's no mystery or twist of fate how adoptive parents take to parenthood, because they want it so much. The question of what is family isn't a matter for tortured debate and self-analysis for them. They know and they're right. When an adoptive mummy and daddy want you so much, are prepared to jump through all the processes, hoops and hurdles, there is an alchemy, an alchemy of nature itself, and, for most, a family with unbreakable bonds through life and death. Mum and Dad's focus in life was Fiona and me. They worked hard and they made sacrifices for us. They lived for us and I know would have died for us. Their maternal and paternal instinct was the same for me as it was for my sister, their birth daughter, fortified by an all-enveloping, unconditional love.

Whatever is nurture or nature confounds and defies the simple neat answers an adopted child needs. Families transcend those boundaries. Lives lived together define us in so many different ways. What would my life have been like had Stella kept me? Apparently her sister offered to look after us. Who would I have belonged to then? How would my bipolar have manifested itself? Would I have yearned for another life, fantasised about having a father at a time

213

when the nuclear family was the only morally acceptable option? And whether Stella had kept me or her sister had taken us on, who would I have been then? Maybe I'd have had none of the inner conflicts, and doubts about being an imposter in my own life, that have so defined my sense of self. But somewhere, I suppose I have always known that I'd rather have had them, rather have gone through the mill of self-loathing and crushing sense of rejection, because I know that I got by far the best deal: Mum, Dad and Fiona – my family. And I see now, perhaps because Stella's letters have quietened the inner turmoil, that being and feeling an imposter has been a small price to pay for a life so fortunate.

I've got to a point where it's good being me. Thanks to my mum, dad, Fiona, to Tina, my daughters, Esther; thanks to my diagnosis, to the many, many adopted children I've met working on *Long Lost Family* over the past eleven years; to working through the labyrinth of adoption and to reading Stella's letters and truly finding her when I opened and read them thirty years after she sent them.

And, of course, thanks to my best friend in the whole wide world, the one who helped me get rid of the clutter, clear my mind and elicit all of these simple truths. To be my real self and my best self. My therapist with four legs, a forthright tail, and the most beautiful brown eyes. The one who knew nothing but understood everything. The one who convinced me that there's no need to pretend, no need to hide, and no need to overthink it. The one who said nothing. The one who shone a light on my childhood and helped me understand it. How could he, Maxwell, ever have been in any other family but ours, been anyone else's dog but mine?

Maxwell helped me to be me, to face up to the imposter, as much as anyone or anything. Time with Maxwell meant the nonsense was gone, the din silenced in our haven of carefree contentment. We both knew it would be like this from that first day as I got down on the floor to welcome him. I'd been waiting for him since I'd lost my first-brother-in-legs, Candy. I've never forgotten that little dog and how much we loved each other. I've never forgotten how he was at the centre of my world, how, while I'd made Mum and Dad's family complete, he'd made mine.

And all these decades later, I owe so much to Maxwell. Our relationship has been one of total trust and under-standing and when we're alone together in enhanced solitude the feeling of peace he brings, the golden compan-ionship he gives me, is indescribable. Walking the hills and beaches together, both knowing exactly where we're going, even on a route that's new or a mountain never climbed, he runs ahead, lost in the forest, then pops out two hundred yards ahead and looks around for me. He spots me, his ears flap back in happiness and he gallops towards me for a reunion as magical as the last one, twenty minutes before. It's like seeing love in constant renewal, powerful and pure. How can that not make anyone the best that they can be? These are the best of times. Unlike with so many animals who suffer or are tortured and exploited, orphaned and abandoned, I have been able to cherish and protect him, to never have abandoned him. Sometimes, as I look into his eyes, I wonder how I lived for thirty-five years without a dog. But then, he wouldn't have been this dog.

Maxwell is an old dog now and we're like two characters in one of those 1950s adventure films, bonded at the end because of what we've been through together. While it's by no means the end for either of us – hopefully – we've come so far and been through so much together. Maxwell gave me back to myself – unadorned, unvarnished, unspoilt. The only me he knows is the very best one – no affectations, worries, anxieties or jealousies. Only me. Maxwell has brought me home.

At twelve, he's younger than all the kids in human years, but older than me in dog years. Figure that one. He still has his crazy moments, but he's more measured, more thoughtful. Wiser and calmer. I guess we both got there together. And boy, does the boy know where he belongs. He's one of the family and like me, he always will be. He's still teaching me things, and I'm still learning. Always learning. Still a little boy playing with a dog on the carpet.

Mum and me, with Dad looking on, 2018

EPILOGUE

Mum

ON 16 DECEMBER 2019, AGED ninety-six, Mum died. She was active, bright as a button, still driving here and there, busy and involved, and then her liver began to stop working. For a few weeks she was in indomitable good humour, doing her crosswords, reading and sleeping in Perth Royal Infirmary, close to Fiona and Ray. We'd think she was going downhill but then she'd rally and, in her inner steel, show an extraordinary ability to smile and see the best of her situation. She lit up any room that had the privilege of her being in it. On one visit, when we left the ward, I turned round and she'd fallen straight back to sleep again and I realised that the effort she'd made for us had exhausted her.

For the very last chapter of her life, Fiona and Ray took her to their home in their tranquil Perthshire village. They gave her special care, a special chair, a new crossword book and tons of love. She was in no pain, just more and more exhausted as her liver function declined.

We still all thought she would be around for ever. Up to visit her, as she sat in her chair and between snoozes, she would reach for a pen and paper so she could design her future granny flat, which she asked to be built adjoining the cottage. As I was leaving for London, she made a video message for Tina and the girls, told me she was looking forward to the Grand Prix and that Lewis Hamilton was still her favourite, and gave me a hug. In that delicate way in which you don't want to say goodbye goodbye, I desperately wanted to tell her she was the greatest mother in the whole wide world, but that was too final. Like a full stop. So I just said, I love you.

The following Wednesday, Fiona rang. Mum had gone and my sister had held her hand as she left. Fiona and Ray had been amazing, caring for her with such love and dedication in her last weeks. It was, in the end, a 'good death', but it hit us all so hard, the devastation overwhelming.

She was our mother, grandmother, mother-in-law, a reservoir of wisdom and experience. Her voice is in every room, her presence everywhere and her love in all of us and if I heard her now, I'd answer before thinking. In an experiment conducted on a large elephant herd into their inner life and self-awareness, their intelligence and memory, scientists played the call of their dead matriarch over a loudspeaker. On hearing her, the herd, and even elephants beyond the family, were thrown into confusion and inner turmoil, not knowing where to look or what to do.

The ethics of causing animals undue stress aside, the results were unsettlingly moving. All their individual relationships with their departed matriarch were disinterred. And a few weeks after Mum's death, I came to experience that same moment, the seconds preceding logic, the seconds before you can rationalise your mother's voice as viscerally transporting to you as her baby's cry is to her.

I was going through some home-movie footage of us all together in Scotland taken the summer before she died. I'd left it running as I nipped to the study to get my glasses. As I picked them up from my desk, I heard Mum's voice and for a few seconds I was so transfixed, I couldn't move. Mum, and red wine, were booming through the room in glorious combination, just as it often was during long Sunday lunches in the Highlands. 'I'm so *cross*,' she was saying, more frustration in her voice than fury. 'When I'm dead, I won't be here to find out what happened. Find out how everyone's getting on.'

'Oh Sheila, you'll know,' said Tina 'you'll be up there, looking down on us.'

'Well,' Mum said, with mock weariness, 'I don't believe any of that stuff, but if you want. Okay. Very well then,' and then plates were cleared and the clatter resumed.

So much one of our family, Mum was lamenting the fact she wouldn't be around to experience the untold future of her grandchildren, the unknown paths of their lives. This to me, was a moment in which I stopped to think of the natural legacy of the day I arrived home and our family was complete. And as I went back into the room to look at more moving pictures of Mum, it struck me, in that light-bulb way that switches on for the recently bereaved, that she will always be a part of my future and, more importantly, my children's future. Her family will go on and as such, she will be part of their lives for ever. When their children ask about Mummy's granny, they will have such a wonderful woman to conjure from their memories.

Mum's funeral took place in January 2020 on a beautifully crisp Edinburgh morning, fresh after the overnight rain. Tina, the girls and I were staying in my parents' favourite old hotel a couple of miles from my childhood home. I hadn't really wanted to stay there because it was all too raw – and there weren't enough beds for us – but in the early morning I'd got up and run along the streets of my childhood to the home I'd always known. I experienced a collage of moments from my life along the way: there was Dr Cameron's surgery; here was the house where Iain and I called five taxis to; that was the road towards Robert's house; that was where Dad washed the car; that's where I walked hand-in-hand with Grand Pa. And as I drew in the sweet scent of the drying pavements, the petrichor, the damp hedges and wet soil, I was flooded with an aching sense of nostalgia. When I got to the house, I came to a sudden halt and stared up the short path from the road. This is where I belong, I thought, and I walked up and stood at the door I'd first come through fifty-eight years before.

This lovely terraced house was Mum and Dad's pride and joy and was, even now, crammed full of their lives. Bills from the sixties, Christmas card lists, cards, long letters, short letters and their love letters. The traffic roared up and down the main road behind me and I leaned my head against the door and a myriad of memories, smells, textures and sounds filled my soul.

Later, at Mortonhall Crematorium, family, friends and colleagues came together from all over the country. Maybe Ray's niece Robin summed it up best as she took my hand and told me: your mother was a remarkable woman and I am privileged to be here today to send her off. And for a friend who hadn't met her, yet knew her story, knew so well about what she had done for me, it was, she said, one of the most poignant but joyful funerals she'd ever been to, that of a loving and deeply loved mother – to her, the greatest tribute on earth.

The humanist celebrant was superb – thank God – summoning Mum's life and times, painting her portrait with dignity and blessing. Through my tears, as I glanced around the congregation, I could see a comforting array of faces, a tableau of my life and times; places and feelings, as if this was the point of arrival and everything had been leading up to this moment. The final act in the play when all the characters come together and the inevitability of this moment made sense.

It truly was an extended family celebration of her life. Robin sang 'Edelweiss' from our family's favourite film, *The Sound of Music*; and his niece Alison, a professional musician, played Bach's first cello suite. All my girls went up, heartbroken but staying as strong as they could. They did their beloved granny proud. Lilla and Kirsty read the poems they had chosen, Isla played her flute and Breagha fought back the tears to share her beautifully measured tribute to her granny, so full of everything she meant to her. Twenty-one years before, when she was born, Mum had come down to help look after her and their bond had always been strong and constant, right up until her death, when Breagha had become a student at Edinburgh University.

In the day before the funeral as we all worked out what we were going to do, Breagha wouldn't tell anyone the piece she'd chosen to read. As she stood at the lectern fighting back the tears, she told everyone how Granny had been such amazing company and comfort as she got used to university life. They spent many an evening together watching soap after soap, talking about life and enjoying her comforting 'spag bol'.

Then Breagha took a breath and the words of Robert Burns stopped all the clocks and it was perfect.

> Few hearts like hers, with virtue warm'd,
> Few heads with knowledge so informed;
> If there is another world, she lives in bliss;
> If there is none, she made the best of this.

During my eulogy, I felt an overwhelming sense of belonging, so proud to have been her son, seeing now the happy, sad faces of all whose lives she'd made better for being alive. As I brought her back to life with stories and memories, there was a roar of laughter as I mentioned her good humour right to the end. In the hospital, when a nurse was running through a standard questionnaire, Mum answered dutifully. Religion? None. Gender? Female. Recreational drugs? If only.

When the casket was taken away, I felt a hit of panic. Mum and Dad both gone, now it was over. That is such a moment in life. The photograph we'd chosen for the back of the order of service showed the two of them coming out of the church in to the bright future on their wedding day, both looking as happy as any two human beings could ever look. The moment captured by the photographer was their love. A love that I'd had all my life. Fiona had found some love letters to her from Dad, which we'd placed on her funeral casket so he could tell her how much he loved her one more time.

This was our life. Fiona and I had discussed the eulogy and I was delivering both our words and as I saw her willing me on, I hoped I was doing okay – for her and for our parents. I belonged there, Mum's son, paying her tribute on behalf of me and my sister. Pride and grief made me invincible and in the truth of those moments the imposter was a distant, forsaken figure.

In a wonderful piece of symmetry, a couple of years earlier Mum and I had made a TV documentary together about her service as a radar operator during World War Two and, in particular, her role during the D-Day landings. It was part of a week-long series of programmes on the theme of women in war and she had been as insightful and articulate as ever, poignantly so considering the innocent lives lost under those bombs. For whatever reason, she had never received her service medal at the time and so at the end of the programme, at the Royal Air Force Museum in Hendon, she was presented with it at last, a moment to cherish. When Isla, Tina and I had arrived to meet her there earlier that day, she was char-acteristically ebullient, and her words will always stay with me – with all of us – son, daughter-in-law and granddaughter

– as she raised her hand and waved. Hello Family, she said with a smile, words that meant the world to me.

At the end of the funeral service we played the sound from that part of the programme, the closing scene. 'What a wonderful way to end,' she said as at last she received her service medal. And then we played her out with an old favourite: Nat King Cole's 'Smile'. As her best, lifelong friend, Joanna – too poorly herself to be able to come on the day – had told me: 'She was a rare sort, your mum.' A perfect description of the best woman I have ever known.

As the service ended, I nipped ahead of our guests to stand alone in the January sunshine for a few moments. Ahead of me was a man walking quickly towards the gates. As if sensing me, he turned, but didn't quite stop completely. A man in a hurry, I thought, moved that he'd made the effort to come, rushing to catch up on the urgency of the after-noon, as touched as if he'd come up from London.

I lifted my hand. 'Thanks so much for being here today,' I said. 'We really appreciate it.'

'Your mother was a remarkable woman,' he replied and I felt that familiar swell of pride that he called Mum my mother. And as I watched him hurry towards the car park, his smart tartan scarf round his neck and hands in his coat pockets, I knew instinctively that we were thinking about the same man, a man without whom neither of us would be there in that moment. I'd realised what I already knew – because he was the image of his father – this was Angus Cameron, Dr Ronnie Cameron's son.

In that brief interaction I'd heard the calm in his voice, clocked his urbane demeanour, his warmth and wisdom, that twinkle in those eyes I'd known all my life. If it hadn't been for Ronnie telling Dad about the selfless woman from Ireland, this would have been the funeral of just another stranger. I thought about running after him but my family were coming towards me, the chapel emptying, and I needed to stay where I was. 'And your father was a remarkable man,' I thought, watching Angus pull out of the front gates. 'He too gave me life.'

The final time Mum had been able to come and stay with us in London, she was sitting in her favourite seat at the corner of the sofa: gin and tonic, crisps and dips, crossword and *Coronation Street*. Maxwell and I were lying on the carpet as I tickled him and he sighed with pleasure, pulling my hand back with his paw if I slackened.

Mum looked down on us and smiled: 'Just like you and Candy playing on the floor,' she said.

'I don't know what I'd do without him Mum,' I replied. 'I dread the day,' she said.

'Remember the day Candy died?' I asked.

'Oh I do. So well. It was terrible,' she said, looking over at Maxwell. 'You've got such a friend there.'

As we were talking, Maxwell saw his chance, leapt onto the sofa and snaffled her entire bowl of crisps, like a wolf would a wildebeest. Friends can sometimes be terribly embarrassing, but what the hell, we still love them.

When I have a grandchild or two on my knee, they may ask about my mum and dad, what they were like. 'The best in the whole wide world,' I will tell them. 'I had two mummies. One had me in her tummy but she wasn't able to look after me. She was a very kind and caring mummy, and made sure I went to a good family. Then I got a new mummy and daddy and sister for the rest of my life. My new mummy was called Sheila. Great Granny Sheila. I was very lucky to have her as my mum. She was my adoptive mum but she was my real mum.'

Acknowledgements

My huge thanks to Jonny Geller and Cathryn Summerhayes at Curtis Brown, and Rowena Webb and the superb team at Hodder.

My remarkable editor Gillian Stern saw the book I needed to write as soon as we talked. She gently encouraged me to go where I never thought I would or could, and pointed me to the very heart of things, however difficult and uncomfortable – and at times it certainly was both.

So many amazing people have told us their stories on *Long Lost Family* with such candour, and now it's my turn. The hardest thing of all was reading my birth mother's unopened letters, and without Gillian they would have remained unopened, in a box in a drawer in a house that didn't know or care about them. She was right. I trusted her and I always will.

Family is everything and I thank Tina and the girls with all my heart. They all bore with me during this process and understood how important it was to me.

Mum died while I was writing this book. We'd had some great conversations as she delved back in time to help me with it. We laughed a lot when she told me about some of my antics with my little dog Candy.

She was the most remarkable woman and we all miss her so much. When we finally cleared her house – the house we had been in all our lives, from my cradle to her grave – I found cuttings, videos and cassette tapes of just about every programme I ever did. She and Dad had always told me how proud they were of me. She may not have given me life in one limited sense, but when I look at my four beautiful girls, I realise that she'd given me everything.